HE'S EVERYTHING TO ME

RALPH CARMICHAEL

HE'S EVERYTHING TO ME

WORD BOOKS
PUBLISHER
WACO, TEXAS

A DIVISION OF
WORD, INCORPORATED

HE'S EVERYTHING TO ME

Scriptures quotations are from *The Living Bible,* Paraphrased,
copyright 1971 by Tyndale House Publishers, Wheaton, IL.

All possible effort has been made to give
proper credit and secure permission for
photographs used in this book. Any oversight
will be corrected once it is called to the
publisher's attention.

Library of Congress Cataloging in Publication Data:

Carmichael, Ralph, 1927–
  He's everything to me.

  1. Carmichael, Ralph, 1927– .   2. Hymn writers—
United States—Biography. I. Title.
BV330.C37A34   1986   783.9′092′4 [B]   86-9134
ISBN 0–8499–0094–8

Printed in the United States of America.

6 7 8 9 8 FG 9 8 7 6 5 4 3 2 1

contents

acknowledgments

As I have found out, there is more to publishing a book than just the writing.

But about the writing. . . . I wrote every word of this book in long-hand, filling some three hundred pages of lined, legal-sized, yellow notepad paper, with about fifty misspellings per page and no punctuation. So, a big thanks to my secretary, Lillian Merrill, for deciphering my crude hen-scratchings.

Thanks also to Floyd Thatcher and Ernie Owen of Word Books, who may have given up hope that there would ever be a book, but never once let on.

A very special thanks to Dick Baltzell of Word, who stroked, threatened, inspired, and bugged me to keep writing.

Thanks also to Anne Christian Buchanan, my project editor at Word, who performed many amazing literary feats of derring-do, not the least of which was to organize my half-century of ramblings into chapters and give them titles.

And finally, thanks to my darling wife, Mar, who proofed and spoofed her way through each torturous chapter, putting up with my Hemingwayish delusions.

Oh yes, allow me a P.S. "thank you" to all the Word Books sales representatives, who kept pre-pubbing this book through the years. I know it's hard to believe, guys, but it's finally done!

overture

Several years ago, I was invited to attend the annual Christmas party of Word, Incorporated, in Waco, Texas. When Jarrell McCracken, the company's president, heard I was coming, he asked me to make a little speech to the Word family.

I readily agreed. But then, almost immediately, I wished I had begged off. I stewed and fretted more over that little speech than if I had been writing a complete, ten-arrangement album.

By the night of the party I had started and discarded about ten different ideas. And that evening, as I sat staring at the festive centerpiece, I still wasn't sure which one I would use. When the emcee introduced me, I went with the latest idea, which I had titled, "Christmases I Remember." It was a chronological recollection of the trials and triumphs of being a boy in the Carmichael household at Christmastime.

The speech went great! And the more the audience responded, the more detail I conjured up from Christmases past, and it's possible that some details may have suffered a certain amount of inaccuracy. But at any rate, I enjoyed myself—so much that I exceeded my time allotment by just about double.

When I finally returned to my seat, Jarrell leaned over and said, "Ralph, you ought to write a book some time." Then Keith Miller, who was sitting at the same table, added something to the effect that, if we had transcribed the speech just delivered, I'd be more than halfway there!

Well, that night the damage was done. Jarrell and Keith had planted the seed of an idea that would not go away, and my ego had been properly tickled by the idea of writing a book.

Oh, I had misgivings, too. All my life I had been in the business of making music, and I wondered if only words from me—without any music—would carry any weight. It also occurred to me that the business of writing a book is a rather pompous undertaking; one seems to assume that one has something to say. Sometimes I felt I did. But then again I could think of many of my peers who had led far more interesting and victorious lives than I and who were not preparing for publication.

So, I did what I do best: I procrastinated. How long I procrastinated and what it finally took to get me going will remain a secret between Floyd Thatcher (Word's editor-in-chief) and myself. But I can assure you that what you're holding in your hand is the product of much travail. In it, I've tried to be both honest and responsible. I've wanted to be revealing, but not irreverent or crass. My hope is that the book will have something to say to as many people as possible. (In a way, it's sort of like writing music.)

I started the actual writing with several messages that I wanted to get across. First, I don't want preachment or high-minded instruction, but rather a sharing of experiences from one who has seen and lived through both good and bad and who (I hope) has come to know the difference between the two. And I want the book to be a statement of my Christian faith. Naturally, that is a gift I'm most eager to share.

In addition to that, I want this to be a book for young people who are dreaming a dream. I'd like them to realize that under the right circumstances their dream, no matter how impossible it might seem to others, can really come true.

Obviously, this is a book about music. But don't worry; it most certainly is not a music textbook or a dusty tome on the subject of music education! What I want to do is replace some untruths with what I believe is the truth and to attack a myth or two.

Above all, I pray that in some small way this book will free people. One of the most beautiful sounds in the English language is the word *free*. The most horrible existence in the world is to be in bondage— to sin, to a system, or to another person. And until we give ourselves back to God, we can never really be free. But when we do give ourselves to God, we are able to see clearly our relationship to other people and to find our place in the scheme of life. Things get into balance; priorities fall into proper place. And that is when we are really free. (Of course, by "free" I surely don't mean irresponsible. The fact is, the freer you are, the more responsible you become.)

I suppose everyone has his or her own formula for dealing with life situations—you know, the doors that open for us and the ones that close. I'm not going to try to sell my formula as the only one on the market. But since it has worked for me, I will, over the course of the book, hold it up for examination.

Simply stated, my formula is this: When you go for something, you will get one of three responses: (1) yes, (2) maybe, or (3) no. So, what you do first is take the yeses and run with them; make the most of them. Then you take the maybes and work on them; if you're lucky, you will be able to convert about 80 percent of the maybes into yeses.

And then comes the fun part. You take the nos and start back over them just as though you had good sense. And if you work real hard and just refuse to give up, you'll probably convert about 50 percent of the nos into yeses!

Obviously, there are situations when continuing to work on those nos is a waste of time, and may God give us all the wisdom to know when those situations occur. Besides, it's always possible He may be the One saying no, so it's important to pay attention to Him through the whole process.

But the point is, the person who gives up after the first no is going to end up with twice as many negatives and half as many positives. This whole notion is pretty well summed up in the old saying, "Don't take no for an answer." It has served me well in matters of both a business and personal nature, and it surely has propelled my adventures in the field of music.

I've often wondered what my life would have been without music. Nothing moves, motivates, or fulfills me the same way, and nothing arouses my curiousity like music does. I can see a beautiful piece of machinery and appreciate what it can do without being the least bit curious as to what makes it tick. But ever since I was just a kid, whenever I have heard a chord or a rhythmic pattern, I have never been able to rest until I have "skulled it out" and duplicated that sound.

There is no other line of endeavor that could have held my attention or exacted the heavy demands on me that my music has. There was a time years ago that I stayed up for sixty hours straight, writing music for a Roy Rogers/Dale Evans ABC-TV variety show while simultaneously arranging and recording an album with Roger Williams! That stunt landed me in the hospital for a couple of days. But I was back for the following week's show—a little bit slower and a whole lot smarter. The point is, I would never have spent that kind of time and effort on something other than music.

I firmly believe you have to like something in order to be good at it. (And I'm making no claims as to how good I am, but I can tell you I like what I do.) And a singleness of purpose is also a prerequisite for success in any field. I have known some very talented people who, because they keep going short distances in many directions, never go the distance to reach any one goal. What a waste! I have known other people with lesser talents who possess a singleness of purpose, and they have the mark of achievers.

But what is talent and what is achievement? What value is a goal or a dream? Perhaps in the mysterious process of maturing, we are allowed to peek over God's shoulder, as it were, and to compare our list of priorities with His master checklist. Then, as we mature, we can rearrange our priorities so that they match up with His. God gives us all the accouterments of life—different measures of varying ingredients. But we all start with something upon which to build. And we are all responsible for building the kind of life He would have us build.

I'll never forget the day I discovered that God could use my foolish music for His glory. I felt ten feet tall. It was as though I heard Him say, "You give me everything you are and have, and I'll give you anything you want." It sounded like the best offer I'd ever get, so we went into partnership.

And that, as much as anything, is what this book is all about. It includes the good times and the bad, the wins and the losses, the bright skies and the dark. Summed up, it's the day-by-day maturing of Ralph Richard Carmichael. To put this all in a book has been a unique experience. . . . . You might say it's the toughest lyric I've ever had to write.

one

THE GREAT GOSPEL CONCERT

I awakened with a start. The sound of rain? No, it couldn't be; it just could not be. . . .

I swung my feet to the carpeted floor and crossed to the window. The sky was dark, even though it was still late afternoon, and there *was* rain—lots of it. From the tenth floor of the Sheraton Universal, I could see the lights of bumper-to-bumper traffic on the Hollywood Freeway. The rain-slick pavement reflected the car headlights, making the freeway look like one long red and white neon snake.

The Hollywood Bowl lay just over the hill to the south, through Cahuenga Pass. On the screen of my mind flashed the scene of bedlam that was certain to be taking place at the Bowl right now. Earlier this afternoon, all had been confident tranquility—the culmination of twelve months of meticulous planning for "The Great Gospel Concert." Now there would be panic. What a difference an hour can make! An hour and a rainstorm.

I had to get back to the Bowl. But for the moment it was a relief to be up here, shut away, left alone to gather my thoughts and decide what to do, what to say. My people had worked so hard; the rehearsal had gone so well.

I thought of the twenty-five staff members of Lexicon/Light (the publishing/recording company I had founded and sponsor of the concert), each with a responsibility for making the Bowl concert happen. And then there was the orchestra, one hundred strong; some of those guys had recorded with me for twenty-five years. And what about the thousands of people who had bought tickets and prayed that this would be a special night? If only Noah could see us now!

The jangling phone made me realize I wasn't as safely shut away as I had thought. It was probably the wake-up call I had ordered before beginning my nap.

"Hello?" It was not the wake-up operator, but it was Ray DeVries, my associate producer, calling with all the calm of the entertainment director on the Titanic! He was backstage at the Bowl, and he began rattling off a list of problems. First of all, it was raining there—hard. The roof of the band shell was leaking, and the music was getting soaked. Several amplifiers had gotten wet and shorted out, and the electricians were on a dinner break and nowhere to be found. The outdoor seating area looked like a swimming pool. And, by the way, we had no "rain-out" insurance. "What are we going to do?" he asked.

I didn't answer for a couple of seconds—for the simple reason that I didn't have an answer. It was not a multiple-choice situation. We either had to call off the concert or to go straight ahead with it. And we had to decide immediately—or rather, *I* had to decide immediately. This time I would not be allowed the luxury of passing the buck.

Somewhere from my past accumulation of "trust experiences" came a confidence beyond my weak self, and I heard my voice saying, "Ray, let's go full steam ahead. Find out where the stage hands and electricians go for dinner and send someone after them. Put tarps over the music stands and large instruments. See if you can get the maintenance crew and ushers to sweep the water off the seats once the rain lets up, and tell the musicians to get dressed. This thing will blow over. It *has* to blow over. We've got two hours before the downbeat, and everything will be OK. Just get everybody in gear."

Although Ray was a man of great faith (I called him Lexicon's resident theologian; he was an ordained minister on pulpit leave to head up our company's Special Services Department*), there was silence on the other end of the line. But not for long. Ray affirmed my decision and signed off, saying he had things to do. I said I would get dressed and join him at the Bowl as soon as possible.

Hanging up, I walked to the bathroom and began lathering my face for a shave. I made eye contact with my reflection in the mirror and carried on a silent debate as to the merits of changing blades in my safety razor. The concert that night was something I had dreamed about for years, and now God had let it rain. Who needed a shave

* It was a loss to all of us when Ray passed away in 1982, after this chapter was first written.

anyway—much less a close shave? No one would know or care. I picked up the dull razor.

Then the eyes in the mirror caught me: "But we'll know, won't we?" I fished a new blade out of the murky depths of my travel kit and felt better immediately.

Minutes later, I was pushing the down button for the elevator and checking myself out in the full-length mirror beside the door . . . Bow tie, new tux, cummerbund, patent-leather shoes, and the closest shave possible. "Dear Lord, I've given it my best; I hope you'll do the same."

The elevator door opened, and what a coincidence! I stepped in alongside Cy Jackson and Steve Bock (Word Records sales representatives for the state of California), each dressed in a tuxedo and each forcing a grin.

I said, "Where are you all headed?"

And they answered, "The Great Gospel Concert."

Well, I knew I'd have at least two enthusiastic supporters in the audience. We crossed through the lobby, gave the attendant our claim checks, and waited for our cars in silence, except for the rain . . . it made a lot of noise.

The Great Gospel Concert had been a long time in the making. For years I had mulled over the notion of producing a major celebration of gospel music. We had some of the finest artists in the world on the Light Records label. And what a thrill it would be to get them all together on one stage, at one time, for a great festival of praise!

But I knew that if the concert were ever to be a reality, I would have to do more than dream about it. So one night, flying back to California after a music workshop on the East Coast, Ray and I had started laying the plans.

We had given ourselves over a year to prepare. We would have a staff meeting and assign the various jobs to various committees, each chaired by a Lexicon executive. Everybody would be responsible for something. Every two weeks we would all meet, and the committee heads would give progress reports. The Hollywood Bowl had to be booked, the advertising campaign laid out, the artists chosen and secured, the programs designed and printed, the ticket sales organized and monitored, the orchestra hired, new arrangements written, and parts added to existing arrangements.

The evening had been planned to cover a broad range of gospel music so there would be something for everyone. The program would include soloists, small groups, choirs, and instrumental music. The music itself would range from traditional to contemporary, with quite a few shades in between.

I don't believe I have seen a group of people before or since work together so well as did our staff and artists at Lexicon/Light. It still amazes me to think about it. We came from varied denominational backgrounds, with differing musical interests and, in the natural, little in common. But given a common cause (sharing the gospel through music) and a challenge (the impossible task of filling the Bowl) we combined to form a greater, more noble, entity.

Over a year's worth of hard work had brought us to this September evening with every detail accounted for. The last report from the box office had been "Sold Out." So it goes without saying that a great sense of expectation had filled the air. Until now. I wondered how our little team would handle the rain.

I've always liked rain songs, especially the one that goes, "Here's That Rainy Day." But on 24 September 1976, I wouldn't have given you a nickel to own 100 percent of the copyrights of all the rain songs ever written.

The windshield wipers were fighting a losing battle as I pulled onto a freeway to join a seemingly endless string of blurred headlights. What would normally be a five-minute trip from the hotel to Hollywood Bowl promised to be a start-and-stop headache. The traffic was inching along at a crawl; I figured the slick highway had been the cause for no telling how many fender-benders up ahead.

I knew this was going to take a while. So, getting as comfortable as possible under the "formal dress" conditions, I settled back and turned on KFWB, an all-news station. And then I sat there thinking about how perfect things would be if it were not for the weather and being trapped in that confounded traffic.

Physically, I felt fine, despite the fact that I had written through the previous night, putting the final touches to the music we had spent the afternoon rehearsing. I've gone to hundreds of recording sessions with little more than a catnap and a cold shower. I mused over how delightful the forty-five minutes of sleep had felt, and I smiled to myself at the ironic fact that I'd always slept best when it was raining. (My dad used to say that, too. Come to think of it, he probably passed it on to me.)

I reflected back over the afternoon. What a magnificent orchestra! All my favorite players: nine brass with John Audino on lead trumpet,

Lloyd Ulyate on lead trombone, and Tommy Johnson on tuba; five woodwind players with twenty-five instruments among them, Harry Klee on lead; the six best French horns in the world, with Vince DeRosa playing first; a superb rhythm section that could play anything from "legit" to swing to rock. (What a pleasant surprise when Dean Parks had accepted the call to play guitar. Though he's my son-in-law, I could rarely get him. My daughter, Carol, must have put in a good word.) Then the strings, my wonderful strings—thirty-two violins, sixteen violas, sixteen cellos, and ten string basses laying the foundation, with Jimmy Getzoff as concert master and Bob Stone on first bass. Cap the whole thing off with three percussionists and two harpists, and you'll understand why Hy Lesnick, my orchestral contractor, wanted four-and-a-half months to put out the call . . . not just one hundred men and women, but the *right* hundred men and women.

The rehearsal had gone well. I had fallen asleep convinced that the concert had all the earmarks of being memorable. And it was turning out to be memorable, all right, but not the way I had planned.

My mom would have her own special way to handle this, I thought. She would say, "Just ask Him right out: 'Please God, stop the rain!' Amen!"

The man on the radio was giving a weather and traffic report from the KFWB helicopter. He said that traffic was bad and the weather was worse. I could have told him that without getting up in a chopper! Then he was saying something about the Hollywood Bowl, and I gave the volume knob a sharp twist. "There seems to be a break in the clouds over the Hollywood Bowl. I'm sure that will be welcome news for the sponsors of The Great Gospel Concert, which I'm going to try to attend tonight. . . ."

The rain was still beating hard on my windshield, but I believed!

Then, as I crept closer to the exit which would take me to my destination, I made a discovery that virtually broke me up. The dawning came by degrees. First, I realized that in the last thirty minutes I had not come across any of those two-car huddles on the freeway shoulder that usually earmark the aftermath of a fender-bender. Second, I observed that most of the traffic was crowding toward the Bowl freeway exit, the same as I. Then when I crested the off ramp and got a view of the Bowl entrance, it suddenly hit me that beyond a doubt these people—lots and lots of people—were all headed for The Great Gospel Concert! And the rain really was letting up!

Suddenly all the apprehensions disappeared; the uncertainties were replaced with an uncontainable confidence. I wanted to see somebody or anybody that knew of the near-tragedy we had just experienced. As I parked the car and headed for the backstage area, I kept repeating out loud, "Thank you, Lord. Thank you very, very much!"

The stage was a beehive. Bowl technicians and stagehands, Lexicon staff and orchestra personnel, artists with their managers and entourages, Bill Cole and the sound engineers, Jimmie Baker (our producer) and the lighting crew, the press and well-wishers all were moving back and forth, up and down, and sideways with the precision (but not the grace) of the University of Michigan marching band at halftime in the Rose Bowl. I got in step with a line surging in the general direction of the dressing rooms. I was hardly noticed, but everybody around me was friendly and happy. Many were downright exuberant. I grabbed the doorknob of the dressing room marked "RC" just in time to keep from being swept past by the momentum of the foot traffic. Inside, with the door shut, it was peaceful and cool. The cool got more noticeable by the second. Then I looked down to see I was standing in a puddle of rainwater a half-inch deep. I thought to myself, "Mister Rain, you don't know it yet, but you've been whupped!"

Moving to higher ground, I found myself in front of a mirror again. Now, I had been going to the same barber for thirty years (Art at Sy Devore's) and all thirty haircuts had been satisfactory, but I couldn't resist the temptation of running a comb over the dome one last time, just to make sure that the bald spot was covered.

There was a knock at the door. But before I could answer, it answered itself. Ray DeVries burst in with "We're going to hold the downbeat for twenty minutes. The traffic is backed up for nine miles in both directions in front of the Bowl, and the people can't get to their seats. It's the only fair thing to do. Besides, the electricians still have one bank of microphones shorted out." And Ray was gone.

Viewed in context, the delay seemed like a great idea, and the short in the mikes seemed like a very small problem. (It got to be a bigger problem later on—the short was never located.) Hair! The more I combed the worse it got. I skirted the puddle and moved to the couch and coffee table to thumb through the eighty pages of score which was to be the evening's overture. My thumbing was nimble enough, but my mind was not.

I left the dressing room and moved around to the wing where Brian Bastian, our offstage announcer, was standing at the microphone. The well-modulated tone of his deep baritone voice had a soothing effect as he said, "That's a beautiful sight out there."

Not being superstitious, I took a peek. What I felt is too private to describe. What I saw I'll try to share. Along the tiered rows of outdoor seats, people were moving—some in formal dress, some in raincoats and carrying umbrellas. Some had already located their seats and were having picnic suppers. Here and there a romanticist ate by candlelight in the growing dusk. On and on they came. Some were waving, some were calling; finally all were settled in.

It was time to start. There was a tympani roll and the announcer said, "Ladies and gentlemen, welcome to The Great Gospel Concert." I walked to the podium and looked into the eyes of members of the orchestra. I thought to myself, "I'm glad I put a new blade in the razor." Then I started the overture. The first song was "Like a Lamb Who Needs the Shepherd."

It has been my experience as a performer that when you give something to an audience, you find yourself assessing that gift from two different points of view. From one vantage point, you can judge the artistic value of your gift in the light of your own ability. You have done your best. You have been true to your convictions; you have given a good gift. This has nothing to do with audience response. This is an inner response telling you you've been faithful.

From the other vantage point, you are able to see how your gift is being received. You are being understood; you are lifting your audience, moving it, making it happy or sad, peaceful or animated. Your performance may be marred by some technical flaw. Artistically, perhaps, you could do better. But for the moment that isn't really important. What matters is that you are communicating as never before. You and your audience are one, and you have wings!

On that magical September night, we all had wings. The response to the message of our music was most rewarding, and the artists gave of themselves in a manner I have rarely seen. Their gifts were good, and the audience received them with exuberant appreciation. God blessed us all.

The Great Gospel Concert ended with all the performers lined across the stage and joining with the orchestra and fifteen thousand spectators in singing the Andrae Crouch song, "To God Be the Glory." His glory had certainly filled the skies above the Bowl that night, bringing to a climax a collective effort I shall never forget.

As the applause died and people made their way to the parking areas, a sprinkle of rain began. Umbrellas popped into bloom as sprinkles turned quickly to a steady rain, and soon the walkways were running with water.

Standing in the wing of the Bowl, watching it come down, I couldn't help but smile . . . tonight I would really sleep.

"Looks like we're in for a good one," observed a stagehand standing nearby.

"Sure looks like it," I answered. Then to myself I thought, "When will I ever learn to trust Him?"

two

RAISED IN A CHURCH PEW

I was saved probably about one hundred eighteen times before I reached puberty. Now, I'm only kidding, but the fact is that every time I sat through a hellfire-and-brimstone sermon (and I sat through a lot of them), I was the first one out of my seat when the invitation was given.

I was born in a Christian home. My father was an Assembly of God preacher and pastored three congregations during the eighteen years I lived at home. (We lived in Quincy, Illinois, until I was six; moved to Fargo, North Dakota, until I was twelve; and then moved to San Jose, California, where I finished high school.) My mother was a Bible teacher and actually the better speaker; she could make the Bible more exciting than "I Love a Mystery." My grandfather, three uncles, and five cousins were preachers, and I grew up watching new churches being built.

In my life, I have seen faith and I have seen disbelief. I have seen lonely people with broken hearts. I have seen human terror and fear and evil you could shake hands with. But I have also known God. And when I write about Him in a song and say He was there and did such and such, believe me, He was where I said and He did what I said. His love is real, and His Son is the Savior of every person who will put their faith in Him.

I don't believe that I was your usual, run-of-the-mill preacher's kid (PK); I really wasn't that bad. (I got bad after I left home.) Likewise, my father was not your usual preacher (at least not the way preachers are often stereotyped); he was not that straight-laced. As a matter of fact, my mother terrorized the denominational leaders with her stylish clothes, fancy hairdos, jewelry, and makeup. And Dad just ate it up.

A funny thing I noticed in those days was how most of the preachers who would never let their wives get "gussied up" sure did a lot of mooning and palavering over somebody else's woman who was. Then they'd get right back up in the pulpit and preach against makeup.

I'll never forget a certain evangelist who held a revival meeting at our church in Fargo, North Dakota. He took a fancy to my fiddle playing, and Dad thought it would be good experience for me to go with him to Minot, North Dakota. So when he left our church to start his next series of meetings, I went with him. The bargain was that I would practice during the day and then play in the services at night.

Now, this guy was younger than Dad. He was extremely demonstrative in the pulpit; he growled and perspired a lot. And he was dead set against women wearing makeup. Out of the pulpit, he was not very nice to his wife. Actually, she could have been a very beautiful lady, but he kept her pale as a ghost and sanctified from head to toe.

One day, the circus came to town, and this preacher asked me if I would like to go see the animals. Wow! Was he serious? I'd like to go anywhere to see anything just to get out of practicing that violin! So off we went—just the two of us (he said his wife wasn't feeling well and didn't care much for animals, anyhow).

He parked the car and went through the turnstile, with me tagging right behind. He was looking this way and that and suddenly must have seen what he was after, because he cut between two tents and went to the rear of one particular tent. I heard giggling coming from under the flap, and he stood there combing his hair, just as he did before going into the pulpit. When his long, black hair was pompadoured just right, he lifted the tent flap and cooed, "Well, hello, girls—I must be lost."

One of the young ladies made a quick move for a silvery-looking object, which turned out to be a galvanized slop bucket. I heard "swoosh," and she caught him just under his chin with the full load. I never did get to see the animals, but I somehow felt satisfied just the same.

In all fairness though, that man was an exception. In fact, some of the most fabulous people who occupy the gallery of my memory are the evangelists and gospel musicians who were house guests in the Carmichael home and pulpit guests in Dad's church.

Some of those guests made me think about things beyond my years.

For example, there was one preacher who spoke at Dad's church in Quincy, Illinois. He was so serious and so awesome in the pulpit that he could scare a congregation to death. The fear and dread was so thick you could almost touch them. Everyone seemed to be miserable with guilt and apprehension. Handkerchiefs would come out and tears would flow. I was sure that nobody in our church would ever smile again.

Now, the rule in our house was that if I had to go to school the next day, I had to head for bed the minute church was out. So that is what I did the night that evangelist preached. Then I lay there in the dark worrying about how sad everyone was and how hopeless life in general seemed to be.

The parsonage was right next door to the church—not more than twenty-five feet away. I was upstairs in the second bedroom. Pretty soon I heard low voices. That meant that the last parishioner had left the altar; the lights had been turned out and the church door locked; and the evangelist, Dad, and Mom were covering the distance on the brick walk between church and home. When I heard the old spring on the front screen door do a friendly "wang," I knew I wasn't alone any longer.

I heard them come in and whisper their way to the kitchen and then back to the dining-room table. Then I heard the click of spoons on the ice cream goblets and the glug, glug, glug of Canada Dry® ginger ale. You see, vanilla ice cream doused with ginger ale was a regular grownups' ritual after church. It always seemed that the longer the church service ran, the more ice cream and Canada Dry® it took to settle everyone back to normal.

That night, I kept straining to hear what was going on. And what a relief it was when finally somebody forgot to whisper and started talking right out loud in a conversational voice. Sure enough, the evangelist was telling a story. Then Mom started to chuckle, and the story got louder. And then suddenly they all laughed and started talking at the same time. The evangelist didn't sound mean or angry anymore. And I was so glad for that. I knew I'd have to think about all he had said some more, because I didn't have it quite figured out yet. But for now I could go to sleep knowing all was well.

There was another evangelist who left quite an impression on me. He wore beautiful suits made out of shiny material, and those suits made him seem really important. He was so tall that I had to lean back and look up to see the top of him. His voice was low and booming, and when he talked you just naturally listened.

Well, I had about halfway decided I would like to grow up to be like him. Then one day something happened to change all that. It was the Fourth of July, and a picnic had been promised on the banks of the Mississippi River. My folks had bought me a little red-and-yellow sand pail for the occasion, and I was flitting all over the place, eager for us all to get going. Mom was in the kitchen packing the lunch, while Dad and this hero-type evangelist were out in the backyard, probably just as eager to get going as I was.

Suddenly, this fellow asked if he could borrow my sand pail. That made me proud, and I handed it to him without question. He produced from his pocket a firecracker that looked about a foot long to me. He walked to the middle of the yard and turned the pail upside down over the firecracker, with just the fuse sticking out. He struck a match, touched the fuse, and ran back to where Dad and I were standing. The fuse hissed and sputtered, and then—blam! Up and up and up went my little pail. I did a backbend to watch it pass the steeple of the church, and it just kept going on up. I thought it would never come back to earth, but it finally did—what was left of it, that is!

I took one look at that mangled little piece of tin and burst into tears. My eyes blurred as I turned to locate "Mr. Fancy Pants," so I headed for the sound of his booming voice laughing at my tragedy. I was going in about belt-buckle high with both fists flailing. I'd have gotten him, too, if Dad hadn't caught me as I went sailing by.

Well, that was the saddest Fourth of July I ever spent. I lay awake that night hoping and wondering. I was hoping that some day that guy would get his sand pail blown to smithereens, and I was wondering how a preacher could be so cruel and mean. It would take a lot of thinking about.

Now again, don't get the wrong idea. There were more good evangelists than bad. Who can be the judge? I may have liked some of the bad ones and disliked some of the best. What did I know? I was just a child. For example, there was this one man who used to come to us with his wife every year about the same time. It must have been in the month of March, because he always built kites with me; we would experiment with how much tail to put on to stabilize the frantic zigzagging in the wind. They said he wasn't much of a preacher, but I didn't agree with that assessment at all.

When I was a kid, it really seemed to me that I was spending my whole life in church. And I *was* in church a lot. Wouldn't you say that every night of the week and three times on Sunday is a lot? "Church" was wherever my folks were holding meetings. That might be a tent, a warehouse, an old storefront building—even a jail, Masonic Temple, civic auditorium, or out in the open air at a fairground or park.

You can understand that, to a kid, so much church might get a little repetitious and dull. If you accept that, then you're ready to hear that my favorite occasions at church were those times when a dog—yes, a dog—would find his way into one of these formal assemblies. The entrance of a dog always perked up the proceedings! He would trot down the aisle, and suddenly we would have a real happening.

I suppose it was the total unpredictability that made these occasions so exciting. I've seen dogs sit right in front of the pulpit, cock their heads sideways, and listen. Or I've seen them come right down the middle of the congregation, up and across the platform, and over and out the side door. (I guess that brief kind of entrance was really the best for everybody's blood pressure.) I've seen them lift their legs toward a bench or have to be chased around until they started barking or snapping. Then, when an usher or someone would finally get a good hold on the dog and it would start to whine, everyone would feel sorry for it and would get mad at the dogcatcher!

The only problem with meetings that dogs attended was that once things quieted down it always took a while to get the service back on track again. That would add to the length of the meeting, and I never cared for that particular phase of the "old dog trick."

Every preacher I can remember from childhood, including Mom and Dad, had a number of sermons on the topic of the Rapture and the Second Coming. Well, I was no different from the other kids, or most of the grownups for that matter, and those sermons really got my attention. The prospects of the Second Coming astounded, confounded, and pretty much scared me to death.

There were days when I felt I was more or less ready to go, but there were plenty of others when I had just plain lost the victory, so to speak. On days like that, on the way home from school, I'd begin to wonder . . .what if the Rapture had occurred and the folks were gone? I knew beyond doubt that *they* were always ready. That prospect would eat on me until I'd fairly fly over the last half a block to hit the front door in a sweat. As soon as I saw either Mom or Dad, the heat was off. (It didn't do the trick just to see my sister, Ruthadele, because I wasn't really sure about her always being ready to go.)

Now, if I could not find Mom and Dad after rustling around through the house, I'd tear out the back door to the garage. I wanted that big old six-cylinder Studebaker to be gone! Oh, what a comforting sight it was to see an empty garage. If the Lord came back, I knew He'd just take the folks and not bother with that beat-up old "Stude." So if the car was gone, I knew the folks were with it and running errands or visiting the sick. I do believe that if I had ever found the car in the garage and the folks missing from the house, I may not have lived to write about it.

While I was growing up, there was much talk about heaven. We lived in the "latter days" and the Savior's return was imminent. It was in everyone's conversation and it charged the air with expectancy. It seemed to be the motivation behind the feverish pace kept by my parents as they held more revival meetings and started more churches.

Whenever we had visitors in our home or were guests in somebody else's home, there would generally be two or three open Bibles, and the mood would be bright and festive, almost as if we were playing a game to see who could find the best Scriptures. Many times the verses would be those containing God's promises, and since we lived in the aftermath of the Crash of '29, those promises were all some folks had. Other times, the verses would pertain to prophecy, and then a discussion of how many prophecies had been fulfilled before Christ's return would follow.

While I felt guilty about it at the time, I recall taking comfort in the number of prophecies yet unfulfilled. It just seemed to me that it would be unfair to have to rush off to heaven just yet without being able to grow up and do all the fun things that grownups got to do.

Besides, I didn't think the life we had right there and then was all that bad. Sure, we were as poor as the next family, but we managed to enjoy life, anyway.

Mealtimes in the Carmichael household were always happy occasions. And although money was scarce, we were never really hungry. Looking back, I think I have figured it out. You see, Dad always had a number of families in his congregations who would bring things every Sunday . . . maybe a chicken, country butter, a dozen eggs, some milk, vegetables in season, and so on. So, for Monday and part of Tuesday at least, we had it made. Another ingenious supplement to the Carmichael dinner table was my mother's ability to glorify a mess of dandelion greens picked from any one of several vacant lots around our house. She would start with a pile of greens big enough to feed an army. The flavor came from a piece of bacon or a ham hock, and she'd round out the menu with freshly baked cornbread and real butter, washed down with a couple of glasses of cold milk. When it came to eating, I didn't really know we were poor.

Mom's philosophy for life may have grown out of a portion of Scripture she loved to quote: "Godliness with contentment is great gain" (1 Tim. 6:6). Dad would say, "Whatever you do, do it well . . . and try to make a game out of it." Now, I'm not saying that all of their seeds of wisdom fell on fertile ground, but I grew up watching Mom and Dad loving each other and enjoying to the fullest the good and simple gifts that God gave them. As the days went by, I learned to love and enjoy life just as they did.

Dad liked hiking, gardens, mountains, the ocean, horses, music, and people (though he was awfully shy, I'm told). Mom liked sewing, company, cooking big dinners, dressing up and going places, highly polished furniture, and people (she was not shy at all). And of course, they both loved the Lord and His Word.

I guess you can understand that back then the joys of living just naturally steamed over the windows of heaven for me. And even though I liked hearing about heaven and all, I was pretty well occupied at the moment. Besides, from what I heard, there were only two ways to go there—one was dying and the other was the Second Coming. I was scared to death of both!

Then one day Mom came across something that put a new light on the subject of heaven for me. I must tell you that I was crazy about horses—one of the first words I learned to say was "horsey." Well, Mom found this scripture in the Book of Revelation that says something about all the faithful riding with Christ on white horses. That did it—especially when Mom allowed that they would probably be Arabian stallions. I felt certain that life on earth for me would never include a fine steed, so the prospects of heaven grew suddenly more acceptable for this young'n!

Speaking of horses . . . during my growing-up years you could almost have split my waking hours into two catagories—music and horses. When I wasn't practicing a musical instrument (mostly my violin) I was fantasizing about horses. I collected horse pictures and saved my money to buy every issue of *Western Horseman* magazine.

During the time that Dad pastored the church in Fargo, North Dakota, I spent each summer on one of the parishioners' farms. I loved the smell of new-mown alfalfa, the rustling excitement of the thrashing rigs, and most of all the livestock—cows and horses, calves and foals. Some nights I couldn't get to sleep because I was waiting for the sun to come up the next morning! But somehow I would eventually fall off to sleep, only to be awakened before dawn by noises in the kitchen and the sweet smells of coffee perking and bacon frying. Then I would lie there trying to remember which farm I was on—was it Bernstein's, Olson's, or Jorgenson's?

The last summer we lived in Fargo, I didn't go to the farm. I just stayed home and practiced the violin eight hours a day and thought to myself, "Someday I'm gonna play this thing good enough to make some money to buy me a horse."

Dad understood the way I felt about horses—he felt that way himself. So over the years, when the opportunity presented itself, we'd take a "horse break." Sometimes we'd go to a cavalry remount station in St. Louis, Missouri, watch the horses mill around, and breathe the dust. (Dad had asthma.) Later, after we had moved to California, we'd go see the Peruvian Pasos up in the Santa Cruz mountains.

The last horse excursion we ever went on together was to the old Kellogg Arabian horse ranch in Southern California. What magnificent animals we saw that day! Little did I ever dream that thirty years later the good Lord would let me own Farlo$^+$* , whose sire and dam may have already been romping around the Kellogg ranch at the time Dad and I visited there.

My fascination for horses got me in trouble on one occasion. You see, at that time, kids of my particular religious background were not allowed to go to movies. It wasn't a matter of whether the movies were good or bad; it was just no movies, period. Why, most of the churches wouldn't even let the missionaries show the films they brought back from their mission fields!

Now, I didn't especially agree with this, but I did pretty well play by the rules. So when there would be a film at school (usually a travelogue or a historical documentary), I couldn't see it. You had to have a note from your folks saying it was OK for you to see the movies, and of course I wouldn't even have thought of asking my parents for a note. So, while the movies would play, those of us without benefit of a note would sit in the hall. There were usually two of us—just me and a little retarded girl from the "opportunity class" (that's what they called it). Well, I felt so sorry for her that I forgot to feel sorry for myself!

I remember we sat on a big bench about twenty feet from the auditorium entrance where the film was playing. Every so often, someone would exit to go to the restroom, and in the brief moment that the door was open we could hear the sound. Generally, we paid no attention. But one day I knew the movie was called *Custer's Last Stand,* and

---

* The plus mark signifies legion of merit.

that meant horses! Well, about one minute into the showing someone slipped out, and I slipped in. I had heard the sound of hoofbeats, and I just couldn't help myself.

Fortunately, I didn't get caught, because at that point in time I could still pull a whipping if the transgression warranted one! I guess you would say our household lived by the good old rule of "Spare the rod and spoil the child." Mom's "enforcer" was usually a hairbrush or a telephone cord. Dad's was sometimes a switch, but most often his belt. The belt has a particularly deadly sound when it's being pulled from around the waist through the loops in a big hurry.

At the time, I didn't care a whole lot for your "good old rule." And on general principles I would always plead innocent. But in all fairness to Mom and Dad, I must admit I really can't recall getting a whipping I didn't (more or less) deserve.

Maybe in those days the "good old rule" worked better because it was used with discretion. I don't believe my folks ever had to lose their tempers in order to mete out punishment. It went sort of like this: I was told, "If you do such and such, you'll get a whipping." Well, sure enough, without fail, Dad and Mom would keep their promise. I'd do it, and I'd get it! Then it would all be over, and the love would keep right on going. You remember that line, "This is going to hurt me more than it does you"? Well, I always thought Dad originated it. And you know, I think he meant it!

I want to keep things in perspective here and hasten to say that my sister and I never came close to being juvenile delinquents, and Mom and Dad were never in danger of being pulled in for child abuse. Rather, our home was one in a million. There was lots of love, joy, and understanding; lots of industry, excitement, and fun. And always lots and lots of music.

three

A LEGACY OF MUSIC

Do you want to know why music affects my life the way it does? Well, I'll share with you my very first recollection.

My crib is in the upstairs bedroom. It sits in a corner with a window and a puffy curtain on one side and a solid wall on the other side. A little way along the window wall is a heating grate or register. That grate is my window to the world. When I get out of the crib, I can crawl over and look down on the tops of all the heads that are in the living room. If I put my cheek flat on the grate and get my eye just right, I can see over to the piano, which is where the action usually takes place. After awhile, I don't even have to go over to the grate anymore to enjoy it; I can just close my eyes and imagine what is going on. As long as that register is open, I get the sound, and that's where the comfort is. . . .

Dad and Mom both played piano, although Dad played better. (Mom could only play the notes as written on the music; Dad put in a lot of extras.) They also sang duets. Dad could play the harmonica and the piano at the same time. Mom could join Dad on her unamplified Hawaiian steel guitar.

Some of the songs were sad and slow; some were happy and swingy. I liked them all. They became a part of me and still are today. Hour after hour, night after night, year after year—what a legacy they gave to me!

Dad was born on a homestead claim in Nebraska and, like many fathers of his generation, he really did walk five miles to the little schoolhouse and five miles back, rain or shine. Sometimes, when my courage would sag at having to be left alone, Dad would tell me how his folks would leave him out in a cabin on the prairie for days at a time while they took the team and wagon into Scottsbluff, some thirty miles away, for supplies. Whenever I would get to feeling sorry for myself, I'd think about Dad as a wee lad out there alone, and I'd perk right up.

A feat that always impressed everyone, including my uncles (Dad's brothers), was that while Dad was still in his early teens, he could top one acre of sugar beets in a day's work. He was probably sweating away over those beets thinking, "If I get good enough at this, maybe I'll make enough money to buy a fiddle." And in those days a good barn-dance fiddler could make just as much as a good beet topper and the work was not as hard. That's what Dad wanted to do. And you know, that's exactly what he did.

But then one night Dad got into a little Baptist church somewhere on the outskirts of Scottsbluff, where he was converted. The word *conversion,* I have come to know, means experiencing a complete "turning around" or "heading in a new direction." That must have been what happened to Dad, because he had no previous religious training or Christian influence—not at home or anywhere. He just heard the gospel and said, "I need that." He repented, and God did the rest.

After his conversion, Dad had to give up the fiddle; the deacons in the church said it was the instrument of the devil. So Dad never played his fiddle after he was converted. But he did keep it, in its dusty case, under the bed, until finally it was discovered and he had to come clean and get rid of it altogether.

I don't think it was coincidence that, when I came along, the first thing Dad put in my hands was not a baseball bat or a mitt, but rather a small violin. I believe it was called one-eighth size, but it was a real, playable fiddle.

At age three and a half, I started taking lessons with a teacher from the Georgia Morry Conservatory of Music. The lady must have thought my folks were crazy to want lessons for a child so young. But she went along with them and would come to the house twice a week to show me how to hold the thing under my chin and how to hold the bow. I had to learn the names of the strings and be able to tell her which string she plucked just by hearing the sound.

I wasn't allowed to play any real notes at first, and this drove Dad to frantic despair. He wanted so badly for me to be able to play a tune; I think he just ached for it. Then, finally, the day came that I played a tune—probably something like "Jesus Loves Me"—and all the tension and anxiety went out of Dad as though he had settled a score. Something he had been robbed of he had been able to give to me. And vicariously he was playing that little tune instead of me and saying, "Devil, today I'm destroying your claim to the violin once and for all!"

I'm not saying that all this was conscious on Dad's part; in fact, it wasn't until long after his death that I really saw the connection between his being deprived of playing the violin and my being fashioned in the image of a child prodigy on the instrument. But even in the midst of the Depression, he saw to it that I had violin lessons from the best teachers available. From the time I was three-and-a-half years old until I left home thirty days after my seventeenth birthday, I had a weekly music lesson, and my folks really had to sacrifice to arrange that.

My early repertoire was a mix of simple classical pieces that I learned from the teacher, plus some old hymns and Sunday school choruses that Dad would suggest. Because he had not been allowed to play, he was determined that my violin music would be used in his church meetings. And since the classical pieces wouldn't go too well in church services and tent meetings, he encouraged me to put some embellishments on gospel songs for public use. For example, he'd say, "Play the second verse up an octave higher," or maybe he'd say, "Play the first part softer and slower, and then on the chorus play louder and faster." That's where this whole business of arranging probably got started for me.

As I got older, I'd play "double stops" and "triple stops" (two and three notes at once) on my fiddle. I'd add some arpeggios, scales, octaves, harmonics, and even key changes. Whatever I learned in the classical pieces, I'd find a way to incorporate into the hymn arrangements.

From the time I was four years old, I was "appearing in public"— and dreading every minute of it. A very wise man once said, "We have nothing to fear but fear itself." I wish he had been around to explain that to me when I was a kid. You see, if we had company at our house, whether it was one person or a dozen friends and relatives, I'd have to play the violin for them. Calling me by my childhood nickname, the folks would yell, "Dickie, play the fiddle for the company." When the audiences were larger, they would stand me on a chair so the people could see me better. And of course, I would play during church services, too.

Now, Dad wasn't the only one who contributed to, or got something out of, these performances. Mom was in charge of wardrobe and makeup. Mother was, and is to this day, an expert seamstress, and unfortunately for me, I came along first instead of Sis. I think Mom had always looked forward to sewing baby clothes for a little daughter. Well, the fact that I was a boy didn't stop her; she just had to change the design a little. How wonderful for her that so many people could see me, the mannequin, and ooh and ah over her handiwork.

The suits Mother made for me were called "Little Lord Fauntleroy" outfits, and she fashioned them of silk, satin, and velvet. They were complete with frilly blouses, sashes, and covered buttons. Of course, the pants were always short to show off my pretty, knee-length socks. And just to make sure that I didn't move around and get mussed up, Mom always had me wear stiff patent-leather slippers that cut my heels and pinched my toes. Add to that a fair complexion and some unshorn locks of bright red hue that had been fashioned into shoulder-length, springy, coiled curls, and you end up with one sissy-looking fiddle-playing kid, scared to death of people.

After I grew up, I was often asked why I closed my eyes when I played. Well, I think it started way back in those "Lord Fauntleroy" days as an adaptation of the old "ostrich trick." I guess I thought that if I closed my eyes, I couldn't be seen.

That worked pretty well while I was playing, but it didn't help much while I was being introduced or on those occasions when I had to sing a little song. There I'd be, standing on my chair, exposed to the world in short pants and curls, with Mom whispering in my ear, "Smile." But the signal that always crossed me up was the simultaneous audible and physical command: for a really animated countenance (an ear-to-ear smile with all teeth showing and eyes ablaze with happiness), Mom would get a good pinch of the fleshy part of the back of my thigh and twist while whispering, "Smile bigger."

Sometimes I think the anticipatory panic was worse than the real thing. The preparation time for one of these public soirees was absolutely devastating to live through. The conversation between Mom and Dad was totally different during those times. There would be just a word or two now and then, like a telegram, followed by a grunt or mumble. (Mom usually had hairpins in her mouth.) The sounds and smells of getting ready to go out in public would settle over me like a crushing, oppressive cloud: the clicking of the toothbrush on the basin, the rattle of the water pipes as the hot water sprayed out of the spigot, the swoosh of Mom's dress going on over her slip, the smell of Dad's soap and aftershave and Mom's makeup and perfume. The tinkle of Mom's jewelry going around her neck and wrists would be the last touch. And I always wanted to cry out, "I don't want to go!"

Before I was old enough to dress myself, Mom and Dad split the chores of getting me ready for my little performances. Dad would bathe me and Mom would dress me. Naturally, I was prepared for the sacrifice before they got ready themselves, which left me nothing to do once I was dressed up but sit and wait for the folks. I recall the trapped feeling as the moment I would have to stand in front of people kept creeping closer. It was inevitable and almost unbearable; I could only sit and wait, listening to the sounds and smelling the pungent odors. To this very day, when I am dressing for a concert or some sort of public appearance, there is a strange melancholy that comes over me.

But don't think for a minute that I suffered permanent damage. Oh, the fear was very real and still is, but I learned to control it. In fact, I have come to think that fear may even be a necessary ingredient in performing. Fear, when it is harnessed, can quicken the senses and bring a kind of natural high. It can give a performer a keener respect for this thing that he or she is about to do; it makes the gift more precious and the giving of that gift a most important act.

If you think I hold any grudges against Mom and Dad for my early performing experiences, you're wrong. Looking back, I know now that they were not just stereotypical "stage parents." They sincerely felt I had a measure of musical talent, and they felt responsible to see to it that my talent was given back to God. To them, that meant playing the violin in church, and performing for guests was a necessary discipline to that end.

And then, there were a lot of privileges that went with playing the violin. I was with my parents more. I was a part of their ministry and included in the activities almost as an adult. There were long automobile and train rides across the United States. Things other kids could only know about through history and geography books and pictures, I got to go and see firsthand: the Washington Monument, the Capitol Building—even Lindbergh's "Spirit of St. Louis" at the Smithsonian Institute in Washington, D.C. We boarded Old Ironsides in Boston Harbor, took a trip on a glass-bottom boat to Catalina, went through the stockyards and a slaughterhouse in Chicago. We saw the Redwood Forests, the Great Lakes, the Grand Canyon and Yellowstone Park, all of the great zoos—and the Graf Zeppelin to boot!

Every now and then, we'd go see my mother's parents in a neighboring state. I was about half-afraid of Grandpa Boatwright, but I really admired him, too. He was handsome in a rough sort of way and built like an ox—with a barrel chest and fists like hams. I heard stories of how he was a terror before he became a preacher—always getting into scraps and even brawling in the street. Of course, I only knew him after his conversion, but he still seemed like a holy terror to me. The only difference was that now he was fighting on God's side, and I was sure glad for God!

Preoccupied as he was with winning for God, Grandpa was still nice to me—always gentle and bragging on my fiddle playing. Grandma was sort of little and frail, but plenty tough enough to handle Grandpa. She just adored him and would wait on him hand and foot.

Grandpa liked to cook—nothing gourmet, but hearty country stuff. I recall one morning when, after about an hour and a half of Bible reading and praying with everyone gathered in the kitchen, Grandpa announced that he was going to fix breakfast. Well, he went at it with a fury, and soon the table was loaded with platters of eggs and fried potatoes, a bottle of catsup, stacks of toast with gobs of butter, a bowl of jam, and a big pot of boiled coffee. All of us shuffled our chairs into position, and Grandpa prayed as though God was hard of hearing and he'd never pray again. His voice sounded as if it were coming over a bullhorn, and "Amen" came just as the grease started to congeal. I sneaked a peek at Dad to see him fidget; I knew he liked short prayers and hot eggs.

Well, before I knew what happened, that table was picked over as if a swarm of locusts had hit it. All I got out of it was one measly egg with no potatoes and no toast—and my uncles had kept the catsup at their end of the table!

Grandpa looked over at me and, not knowing my plight, flashed that Boatwright grin and said, "Son, you sure can eat. Look at that plate, Grandma. You can put it away without washing it."

He should have stopped there, because by going on he made a big mistake. "I'll bet you couldn't eat another bite. . . ."

I said, "Grandpa, I'm still hungry."

Well, when I told Grandpa what had happened, he sent one of my uncles to the store after another dozen eggs. I was loving every minute of it. Then I looked at Mom. She was steaming. So I turned to Dad, and he couldn't seem to find any place to look. So I just looked back at Grandpa and smiled.

Pretty soon the eggs arrived. Grandpa started frying, and I started eating. He was enjoying the whole scene just as much as I was. He'd say, "Son, you'd better have another," and we'd go at it again. Then he would say to my mother, "Adele, you're going to have to start feeding this boy more often."

By the time I had finished number six, Mom looked as if she were going to be sick, and Dad looked embarrassed. But I was so proud (and full of eggs) I felt like I wanted to cackle. Then Grandpa capped the whole affair by declaring that I would perform that very night in his revival meeting and that he bet I would play the fiddle like a "house afire" for the glory of God. And all because he had fed me a half-dozen eggs!

Well, I did play for Grandpa, not only that night, but many others. His meetings were always very lively.

I heard Billy Sunday one night in some big city somewhere, and he was quite a preacher. I remember that before he got going, he took off his coat, tie, and collar and handed his collar buttons to Mrs. Sunday—he called her "Ma"—for safekeeping. Then he wound up and let 'er fly; he was all over the platform.

But if it were a contest, I think I'd have picked Grandpa over Billy Sunday. Before he preached, he'd get the people singing in that old, two-beat gospel style and play the tambourine so fast it was a blur. Whatever he did with his hands in between beats, he would always manage to whack the side of his timber-thick thigh on beats two and four while stomping his foot on one and three. He was a veritable one-man rhythm section. Sometimes the platform would get to undulating so that I thought it would collapse. Grandpa would also strip down a bit like Billy Sunday and rush back and forth like he might take off out across the audience. And more than once he split the top of the pulpit with his fists.

Yes, I think I'd pick Grandpa, especially after what happened one night at a tent meeting in Des Moines, Iowa. It was after I had delivered one of those "house afire" fiddle solos, and people were shouting and clapping. Then Grandpa Boatwright got to his feet and announced in his bullhorn voice that right then and there he was going to take up a "penny offering" for me. He had the ushers come down the aisles, told the people to bow their heads, then asked the Lord to make it a generous offering, "Amen!"

He said I would play another piece while my collection was being lifted, which I did. But I just couldn't find high gear for listening to the clink of all those pennies hitting together in the plate. It seemed like the tighter I closed my eyes to concentrate on a good solo, the wider my ears opened to hear those pennies.

I thought that night would never end, I was so anxious to get back to Grandpa's house to count my pennies. While I don't remember the dollar amount, I do remember that they filled a half-gallon dill-pickle jar almost too heavy for me to carry.

That was a great night for me. But a short time later, it led to a temptation that caused my parents embarrassment and taught me a hard lesson. The occasion was a special rally in a neighboring town; many churches from all over the state were represented. They had asked me to play the fiddle, so Dad and Mom had driven me over. There I sat on the platform waiting to play—sort of fidgeting and fighting off a case of stage fright. The man who seemed to be running things was called the district superintendent, and while I didn't know him, he and the folks were on very friendly terms.

Suddenly this brilliant idea hit me, and with a boldness spawned from my recent "penny offering" success, I slid off my chair with my fiddle under my arm and sauntered down to where this head man was sitting. Somebody else was at the pulpit for the moment; I knew that my turn was coming up shortly and that I had better move quickly. So I headed straight for his ear and whispered, "Usually when I play in big meetings like this one, they take up an offering for me."

Well, I get embarrassed just thinking about it, so I'll give you the short version of what happened next: he didn't go for the deal, and I played a lousy solo. Also, it was a long ride home.

I told you about my fear of audiences, but I had another skeleton in my closet—the fear of being left alone. In fact, I recall several occasions when Dad let me choose between the two. The first happened when we were someplace a long way from home and staying in a drab little apartment provided for the visiting evangelist, which in this case was Mom and Dad (and me). We had gone through our "getting ready for church" ritual, and I knew that shortly I'd be in front of all those people.

Well, all at once I started to feel queasy, and with tears in my eyes I burst out with, "I'm not going tonight."

Dad said, "Listen, Bud," (he called me that when he was either clowning around or peeved—and neither happened often) "either you are going to church, or else you can stay home alone."

There it was. I had to choose which fear I thought I could handle. I ended up going to church . . . that time. But it got to be quite a problem for me. If I went with the folks, I had to stand in front of people and play the violin. If I didn't play the violin, I couldn't go with the folks, and that meant being left alone or with strangers.

During his lifetime, my Dad (with lots of help from Mother), pastored five churches—three before he retired and two after retirement. He was never without a pulpit. While he was pastoring in Quincy, Mom and Dad also started several new churches around the state. And they would often travel to faraway places to hold revival meetings and be gone for weeks at a time.

They took me with them a lot. But the services of a pint-sized fiddle player were not always needed, and I got left home a lot, too. Then when my sister came along (she's four years younger than I), we both were left home.

I was always OK during the daytime. But with twilight would come an itch I couldn't scratch. Then, by the time it was full dark, I'd be overwhelmed by loneliness and emptiness. It shattered my world every time my parents said they were "leaving again . . . but don't cry."

Did you ever smell a paper mill? During the summer in Quincy, the mills down along the river would give off a sharp, sweet-and-sour odor that always got to me about sundown. They said it was the moisture in the air and the change in temperature. I'd be sitting on somebody's front porch swing (having left the table without eating), pining over the folks' being gone again.

Well, the combination of the paper-mill smell, the motion of the swing, and a good case of the "poor me"s would make me sick every night. Then, pretty soon it would be time to go up to a dark, strange bedroom with funny-smelling bedding. I'll tell you, it was no fun waking up alone and not knowing where I was. How could my folks do this to me, anyhow?

When Sis came along, the whole situation was even worse for me, because then I had to pretend to be brave, although I knew I wasn't. I'd remember Dad's being left alone out on the plains of Nebraska, and I would slip my arm around Sis and tell her everything was OK. But I was lying through my teeth.

By the time I was six, I had worked my way up to a well-developed fear of the dark. The parsonage was two-storied and my room was upstairs, which would have been fine except that I knew all about the Lindbergh baby kidnapping, which had been in all the newspapers and on the daily news reports Dad listened to on the big old Edison radio. Words such as *ladder* and *second-story window* and the name *Bruno Hauptmann* (which I pronounced Hoffman) tortured my imagination until I couldn't sleep on the nights Sis and I were left alone while Dad and Mom were in church.

Then there was the Ethiopian War, which seemed to last forever. It was also in the news. I'd lie in bed at night and tense up at every noise I'd hear in the streets below, knowing for sure it was the Ethiopian soldiers coming to get us.

I suppose that fears such as mine were part of the normal stresses of childhood. And while I'm no psychologist, I believe those fears, anxieties, and frustrations helped stimulate me to action—always have and probably still do. You might even say that the negatives are just as important to us as the positives.

The more I think about it now, the more I realize how important my music was to me even back there during childhood. It was my outlet; through it I could express myself. It was my companion in solitude, my language in a crowd. It was my ticket to the haven of approval from my peers and elders. And it would eventually be my road of escape from the oblivion of uselessness.

I am certain that I got my broad appreciation and intense curiosity for music from my father. While people all around us were making a big "to-do" about "worldly" music, we were having a hard time defining the word.

In high school I played the trumpet in the concert band and stage band. I played the violin in the orchestra and string quartet. I was allowed to listen to the big bands on radio and even had a small record collection (78 rpms) of James, Krupa, Dorsey, and Goodman.

What I was *not* allowed to do was go to dances. (I never learned how to dance and can't to this day, but my soul has always danced.) However, I did sneak off to the Civic Auditorium in the summer of '42 and heard Tommy Dorsey; then a year later, Stan Kenton. (We were living in San Jose by then.) I never had the slightest feeling of guilt either time, although I did stare at the bedroom ceiling half the night trying to figure out just what made them sound so good.

Meanwhile, Dad was not neglecting the classics. He arranged an audition for me with the San Jose Civic Symphony Orchestra, and I made it . . . barely. I was a little embarrassed at the first rehearsal when the orchestra manager led me to the inside chair of the last stand of the second violin section. Just in case you don't get the picture, let me put it an easier way: If there had been twenty-seven violins in the orchestra instead of twenty-eight, I would not have been in it!

I also took the bus downtown once a week to rehearse with the San Jose State College Symphony Orchestra. I was still in high school, and they made out as though my being allowed to play with them was quite an honor, but I think the real reason I was invited was that they were hard up for fiddle players.

Remember that in addition to all of this there were always private music lessons (trumpet, piano, violin) and always church performances. Now do you believe me when I say the range was broad and the quantity enormous?

I've had trouble all my life with drums and with the Christian music censors. I won't go into that here, but I do have a drum story for you. . . .

There was this man, perhaps thirty years of age, who was a professional drummer. Well, his wife attended our church regularly, and he would come to church with her on Christmas and Easter. In between, she would request prayer for his salvation on a more or less regular basis.

Now, the general feeling in the church was that there was an omission made in the King James translation of Matthew 19:24; it should have read, "It is easier for a camel to go through the eye of a needle, than for a rich man or a drummer to enter the kingdom of God." But one Sunday the miracle happened. The drummer got through the eye of the needle, although the drums did not. While the new convert was seeking other gainful employment, Dad offered to let him store his drum set at our house to stave off any temptation for him to return to his old ways.

You guessed it right. The drums were "stored" in my room, and I spent many a lovely summer eve pounding away to the big-band accompaniment of the blaring radio, much to the dismay of our next-door neighbor, Cyrus Nelson* (and his lovely wife, Peggy), who has finally forgiven me after all these years.

I came by my trumpet in much the same way. One Sunday afternoon a married couple in their thirties showed up at our house for counseling. I kept an eye on the proceedings, which seemed pretty somber, with conversational exchanges in hushed tones. Then, after Dad prayed a rather long prayer, everybody moved out of the living room and seemed to be feeling much better. I'd never seen anybody with "marital" problems before, so I sort of ambled up through the front part of the house and collided with the party where the living room hall emptied onto the front patio.

It turned out that the man had been a former professional trumpet player. I say "former" because he had just left the trumpet business to take a job in a clothing store, with the hope that the new field of endeavor would be more conducive to marital bliss.

I naturally admired a professional trumpet player and was especially fascinated by one who had played in a real "dance band." When I said as much, he asked if I would like to see his horn. (By that time,

* Now chairman of the board of Gospel Light, a major book and Christian education publisher.

we were all headed down the front walk to his car.) He lifted the trunk, popped open the snaps of an imitation-leather carrying case, and there cradled in a bed of blue velvet was the most beautiful golden trumpet I'd ever seen.

The next thing that man said nearly stopped my heart: "Since I'm not going to be needing this anymore, you can keep it for me and maybe learn how to play it." And that's just what I did. Perhaps that's why to this day I especially enjoy writing for brass instruments.

As I've already mentioned, money was always in short supply, and yet my folks managed to give me the best music available. There were always lessons with the finest teachers around. And whenever he could, Dad took me to hear performances by great performers such as Fritz Kreisler and Jascha Heifetz, two of the greatest virtuosos ever to draw a bow.

I was about six-and-a-half years old when posters began to appear around Fargo, North Dakota, advertising a Fritz Kreisler concert to be given at the Armory Auditorium across the river in Moorhead, Minnesota. It was in the dead of winter, and when the day of the concert came, Dad and I bundled up and headed for the Armory.

At the time, being so young and all, I didn't think a thing about Dad not having tickets, much less about Dad not having money to buy the tickets. On the slow drive over the ice-slick bridge, Dad just kept talking about what a great violinist Fritz Kreisler was and telling me that some day, if I practiced really hard, I would be able to play some of the classical pieces we would be hearing that night.

When we got there, instead of going to the main door of the old, oblong, brick building, Dad took my hand and said, "Come on; let's look around." There were two fire escapes—one on either side of the building. The first one looked inviting. However, the one on the far side of the building also showed some promise. There was the dark form of a man standing on the iron-grated, second-story landing. The door to the balcony was open a crack behind him, and his cigarette glowed in the cold night air.

Dad went up two stairs at a time. One at a time was all I could handle. The man at the top turned out to be an usher, and a kind one at that. I don't recall all that was said, but the last part went something like, "Well Reverend, if you and your little boy want to hear Mr. Kreisler bad enough to stand out here in the cold [and listen], it's OK by me. But if someone complains of a draft, I'll have to close the door, so don't open it more than a couple of inches."

Alternating an eye, then an ear, I saw and heard the first half of the concert through the crack in the door, trying to keep warm huddled under Dad's overcoat. The night air was still and crisp, and the music was sweet and powerful.

Suddenly the man was coming toward the door, and I was sure it was the end of our free concert. Instead, it was intermission, and he threw the doors open wide for people to get a breath of air. During this little break in the concert, the man said something that pleased Dad more than just a little bit. I was curious, but Dad just said, "You'll see." And I did see. When the doors were shut after intermission, Rev. Carmichael and his "little boy" were not only on the inside, but sitting in the second row of the center section, better known as "orchestra seats." All the pieces were thrilling, but the only one I remember by name was the last encore—"Caprice Viennois."

On occasion, Dad would manage the price of one ticket, then somehow get me inside as well on his coattail. He loved the works of the great musicians and, of course, had a greater appreciation for them than I did at the time. But those adventures were rich experiences and taught me how to feel music, to think music, to form my own opinions and develop my own appreciation. It is a debt I'll never get the chance to repay.

What Dad also did in a very subtle way was plant questions in my mind. Though he never said it in so many words, I think my Dad had some serious doubts about much of the church music of his time. I can remember his always telling me before I would get up to play the violin to "put your soul into it." I think it was something he felt was lacking in so much of the gospel music.

Well, as time went by, I developed my own opinions. The more kinds of music I heard, the more I wondered about the stereotyped music I heard in most churches. I grew to consider it as weak. Yes, a lot of gospel music was downright embarrassing to me. It was ill prepared and ill performed; there was no standard of excellence. Oh sure, Dad was going to see to it that I was a good violinist, and that I played in church to the glory of God. But what could I do with just one fiddle?

four

A FIDDLE GOES TO COLLEGE

It was time to go. I had said I was going, and we had all decided I should. Finally, the day arrived.

Including uncles, cousins, and grandfathers, the Carmichaels and the Boatwrights had produced seven or eight preachers that I knew of. So, when the time came for me to choose how I would spend my life, it was just sort of expected that I would pursue the ministry. At that time, I had never heard of a "minister of music," so my alternatives were limited to pastor, evangelist, or missionary.

Still, I had committed my life to Christ, and plans had been made for me to go to Bible college to study for the ministry upon completion of high school. So, I turned seventeen in May of 1944, graduated from Lincoln High in San Jose in July, and headed for Pasadena, California, to enroll at Southern California Bible College. Summer school was already in progress.

Wow, what an adventure! I had negotiated my first loan (of many) from Mom and Dad and purchased a 1934 used Dodge coupe—badly used, but it did run. I was the only one that liked the color, and it was obviously not the original paint job . . . sort of like Thousand Island dressing, lumps and all.

The first miracle was that the old Dodge made it the three hundred miles to Pasadena, and the second miracle was that I found my way to the campus without getting lost. I arrived on a Sunday and was in class by Monday morning—scared to death.

The campus of Southern California Bible College was a thing of beauty. Located on a twenty-acre knoll with lawns and hedges and lots of trees, the old buildings were vine-covered and picturesque. To my way of thinking, the setting was more conducive to summer camp than to an institution of higher learning.

Almost from the beginning, I was asked to provide music in some form for the various student gatherings . . . evening vespers, morning devotions, chapel services, or whatever. They soon learned that the new kid could play the violin more than "somewhat," and I never said no.

The fiddle was many things to me. In a social sense, it was my passport out of the land of bondage. It was my protection from anonymity, and I wore it like a sidearm.

In spiritual terms, playing the violin was my way of sharing and communicating what I felt. If the occasion called for a prayerful attitude or a worship experience, I would choose to play an old hymn such as "Jesus, Lover Of My Soul" or "My Jesus, I Love Thee." If the occasion was one of joyous praise, I'd go into a chorus and a half of "Onward Christian Soldiers" complete with double stops, octaves, and cadenzas—adding a little body language on the hard parts and ending with an explosion of sixteenth-note arpeggios. (I must have played that particular selection a thousand times in churches and youth rallies large and small. I even played it at the Hollywood Bowl during a giant Youth For Christ rally in 1945.)

Artistically speaking, the violin provided me with an avenue for creative expression, and what I did with my music in those days could be called early but crude attempts at "arranging." Most of the hymns and gospel songs had lovely melodies and meaningful lyrics. And I would experiment with various embellishments that I felt amplified the message or at least created a "mood" that was descriptive of, or compatible with, the lyric. For example, "Out of the Ivory Palaces" conjured up in my mind's eye the dazzling glory of heaven. And "God Leads Us Along," the first line of which goes, "In shady green pastures, so rich and so sweet," suggested the loveliest of pastoral visions. So with the bow of my fiddle I tried to paint what I "saw." I suppose I arrived at college with two-dozen pieces in my repertoire, among which were, "Deeper in Thy Love, Oh Jesus," "I Surrender All," "Have Thine Own Way, Lord," and "All That Thrills My Soul."

There were so many times when I felt the limitation of expression with just one fiddle, one bow, and one pair of arms. Even playing all four strings at once was not enough. I suppose it was this feeling of inadequacy, along with an insatiable curiosity, that propelled me to involvement in other kinds of music. By the time the fall semester was a month old, I had helped organize a male vocal quartet which, with an occasional change in personnel, stayed together for several years.

I also began to experiment with a mixed quintet. I was more than a little intrigued by the sound of the "Modernaires" (a pop group) and thought how nice it would be if we could use this vocal form in gospel music. (I'm afraid the rest of my known world did not think the idea was so nice. Our early performances were definitely considered "worldy," and consequently were limited to rehearsal halls or Ping-Pong tournaments held on the college veranda.) Since there was no published music for such a vocal combination, I would write the arrangements and teach them to the group. To the best of my recall, these were the first vocal arrangements that I ever did.

The mixed quintet consisted of two gals and three guys. What made the sound unique (at the time) was that the top gal and the bottom guy sang the melody in unison (the sounds came out an octave apart) with the other three voices singing the harmony notes in between. Such a combination has been called everything from "block" or "close harmony" to "cluster writing."

I must tell you that the men and women in those first groups were very dear to me, and to this day they hold a special, warm spot in my memories. We had some great times together. Of course, it was not always fun; there was much sacrifice and discipline. But to see people respond to our music was reward enough.

It was the custom for students who were musically inclined to be invited to sing or play at various churches in the Southern California area, and I began to get my share of invitations. At first they were just to play the violin. Later, I would be asked to bring a group as well.

I believe my first outing of this sort was to a cozy little church in Glendale pastored by a Rev. O'Dell. I was to play for the Sunday evening service, and a brief rehearsal was scheduled an hour ahead of time with the church pianist, whose name was Linnie Claypool. When I arrived with sweaty palms, the choir was just concluding their rehearsal under the direction of a big, tall, handsome man named Ernie Payne, whom I learned sang bass in the Haven of Rest Quartet during the week and directed choir on weekends. I moseyed cautiously down the aisle, and then Ernie was shaking my hand and smiling his gigantic smile. Then he was introducing me to the choir and to Linnie, who was a pretty little wisp of a girl half-hidden behind a rather large grand piano.

It was kind of awkward as I tuned up to have strangers from the choir standing around whispering and ogling, but then I called out a song title and picked a key and away we went. I truthfully cannot recall what song we played—only that it was very soulful and that Linnie was doing some marvelous chords, embellishing without colliding. Suddenly I was no longer aware of the oglers.

I don't know whether anyone else got blessed that evening, but I did. What a kick it was to find someone else who was hearing the same chord changes that I was. I knew I wanted to make some more music with this person. But before the evening was over, I encountered what appeared to be an insurmountable problem. I met Linnie's fiancé, John Olson.

As it turned out, John was anything but a problem. He and Linnie were married shortly after that first meeting. And as invitations began pouring in for Linnie and me to appear at churches and youth rallies around Southern California, John became our best booster. He even provided transportation for us, no matter where or when we needed to go.

Meanwhile, back at the college, I was severely trying the patience of the faculty. It was not that I didn't like my professors. They were great, and I admired and respected each of them. I really believe that I could have become a good student if I had not had so many distractions. After all, I could count, spell, read, and write. And though some doubted my motives, I was genuinely interested in God's Word and in preparing myself for some kind of Christian service. The question was, "What kind of Christian service?"

My life seemed to be very complicated. On the one hand, I felt a scholastic obligation to attend classes and do my homework. On the other hand, the opportunities to make music occupied every waking moment. I would sit in class and daydream about endless combinations of instruments and voices, and I tried out as many as I could.

Sitting one day in a classroom called "Old Testament I" with one eye on the professor and the other on my wristwatch, I thought four o'clock would never come. Casually concealed within the pages of my notebook were five pieces of music manuscript paper with handwritten notes for three trumpets and two trombones. It was an arrangement for the old gospel song, "A Shelter in the Time of Storm." When class was over, a group of us were to rehearse it, and I had just four bars to complete the second trombone part. It would be the first rehearsal for this brass group, and I was more than a little apprehensive. Would the guys be able to play it? Would it sound OK? But what I felt was more than apprehension; it was sheer excitement. I slid the unfinished part out of the notebook and, shielding it with my open Bible, I appeared to be taking notes of what the kindly old professor was saying. Little did he know.

Of course, four o'clock finally did come, and I bounded for the rehearsal hall. Did the arrangement work? Well, parts of it did and parts of it didn't. That's the way it always was. I'd write something and then, when we actually played it, I'd say to myself, "This part is good; I'll do that some more." Or, "This part is fair; perhaps if I make a change here and there, I'll do that again." But, if something didn't come off at all, I'd say to myself, "Wow! That's the last time I'll try that."

As the days went by, there were more and more rehearsals and more and more invitations to churches and rallies. Every weekend was filled, and usually Wednesday nights as well. We would rehearse every lunch hour and after classes. Then, when everyone else was in bed, I would sneak out of my room, back through the basement, and on down past the laundry room to hole up in a little eight-by-ten-foot practice room that was probably the remotest spot on the campus. There I would work on the arrangements for a vocal or brass group—or whatever I was experimenting with at the time. But I'd only do this two or three nights a week, and then only until two or three o'clock in the morning, because breakfast was served in the dining hall at seven o'clock, and chapel attendance was required at eight.

I never got paid for playing the violin during that time. I never asked to get paid. It wasn't like it is today, when you charge a fee or ask for a freewill offering. Once in a while we'd get gas money, and occasionally one of the bigger churches would make a contribution to the college. But it was not as though we'd say, "If you can pay our price, we'll come and play." We just took every opportunity that came along. I've got some precious memories of that first year of college and some of the places we were invited to appear.

There was the popular Eagle Rock Baptist Church, where I heard the first of three generations of McArthurs preach. There was a layman named Ed Johnson who ran the youth group, and every now and then he would invite Linnie and me to come over at six o'clock on Sunday evenings and play a few numbers. Then I'd stay for the evening service just to enjoy myself.

On one occasion, it was announced that "young Jack" McArthur, home for a visit from seminary, was to be the speaker for the evening. So I thought, *Well, let's see how he does.* Now, in our school we were taught that if you had to read your sermons you probably didn't have them down very well. In fact, there was even some doubt if you had to use notes. But that night I heard "young Jack" McArthur read a sermon that really moved me. It seemed to me that he more than likely spent as much time preparing his sermon as I did preparing my arrangements. He later became Dr. Jack McArthur and has been not only impressing me, but also inspiring me, ever since. (Somebody jokingly told him that the best sermon he ever put together was his son, John McArthur, who now pastors the Grace Community Church in Sun Valley, California.)

On another occasion, Bob Bowman, who sang baritone in The Haven Of Rest Quartet and was choir director at Calvary Assembly in Inglewood, California, invited us to play on a Sunday evening and to come early enough to be on their live radio program. That was a real eye-opening experience. They had the best church choir I'd ever heard up to that time, and the broadcast was mostly music, with well-thought-out continuity from opening theme to closing theme. I also really liked the pastor, whose name was William J. Roberts. He was warm and friendly and obviously liked music. During the evening service, he even encouraged me to play an encore, and in my youthful arrogance I immediately perceived him to be a man of impeccable taste.

It was around this time that I first began hearing the initials, YFC. They stood for Youth for Christ. Everyone was talking about the fabulous thing that was happening every Saturday night in downtown Los Angeles at the Church of the Open Door. It was sponsored by YFC, and they called it the Saturday Night Jubilee. Several thousand young people from all denominations met every week in a great youth rally. What a stir it was causing in the Southland; everyone was talking about the fast-paced program with lots of music and lively preaching—all geared to youth! There were names like Hubert Mitchell, Merv Rosell, Dr. Bob Cook, and Dr. Torrey Johnson.

Can you imagine the panic that hit me when a call came through the college switchboard asking me to play the violin the very next Saturday night at the Church of the Open Door? I did four things by way of preparation: (1) practiced a little extra, (2) prayed a little extra, (3) trimmed my own hair with a pair of rusty scissors, and (4) got my only suit pressed and asked for a "hard" crease. I was as ready as I'd ever be.

Saturday night came, and John and Linnie Olson picked me up at the campus and drove in silence to the Church of the Open Door. You could tell there was something going on, because there were no parking places to be found for blocks around. We entered the auditorium and wended our way through the throng down the far left aisle. Halfway down, I stole a glance over my right shoulder out over the main lower floor, then up to the grand circular balcony and higher still to the upper balcony. I saw people, people everywhere—a seething mass of babbling, bobbing faces, mostly teenagers. I think it was the biggest crowd I had seen up to that time.

Things got started promptly and moved along rapidly. There was Rudy Atwood at the piano, and about an arm's length away from me sat the Old-Fashioned Revival Hour Quartet in beige gabardine suits. The emcee and songleader was a tall, gangly, handsomish guy—I'd say he was at least six-foot-six. His suit must have been specially made, because it surely fit him well; and he had the longest, shiniest shoes you've ever seen. They called him Johnny Sheer.

The proceedings at the Saturday Night Jubilee were a little showier than I was used to seeing in church. There was a lot of laughter and a lot of clapping, and that crowd of kids seemed more comfortable than most kids feel in church. But then I realized I was feeling pretty comfortable, too—comfortable and nervous at the same time. I knew I would be introduced shortly, so I played along with the singing as Johnny led the crowd in a medley of popular youth choruses, some of which were new to me. Playing along helped get my nerves under control. And talking to God in a quiet sort of way helped, too. I thanked Him for letting me be there and for letting me see this fantastic thing happening. I also asked Him to move in the hearts of the kids there who did not believe, so that when the invitation was given, they would come forward and accept Him as Lord and Savior.

I thought how natural it seemed to be having fun and tending to serious business all at the same time. And then I was on. Out of the corner of my eye I saw Linnie Olson sliding in behind the Steinway, and I started to play.

You know, I have to scrounge a little bit to recall all of the details about my first visit to the Saturday Night Jubilee, but there is one impression stamped indelibly on my mind. I remember feeling those kids respond to one fiddle and one bow, and I remember having an overwhelming desire to have a hundred fiddles and bows—with brass, woodwinds, rhythm, and harp—so I could stretch out and give them more.

I said, "God, please let me come back someday with a whole band." And one day He did, but that comes later. . . .

five

ADJUSTING

Back on campus there were good times and bad. If I could just conform to the recommended routine—forget the music projects, abide by the rules, go to classes, study, go to bed, go to chapel, be on time in the dining hall, go to prayer meeting—everything would be all right. And I tried—I really tried. I talked to the dean and vowed to change my ways. But somehow I kept getting off track.

The college had a fine music department with voice teachers, piano teachers—a teacher for this and a teacher for that. The head of the department was a very dignified and portly gentleman who spoke with an English accent. But he never spoke to me; or rather, I never spoke to him. However, we often spoke *about* each other, and none too kindly, I fear. I didn't think his department was doing much of anything, and I had the audacity to feel that he considered me a threat.

When I think back on the hostilities I perpetrated, I am most chagrined. I instigated some terrible pranks to embarrass the music department, one of which I'll admit here and relate as best I can recall.

It was the custom at the close of each semester for the music department to sponsor a recital in which all of the music students would perform. They would receive credit on their performance and would be graded accordingly. It really was quite an occasion. There was a very large fireplace at the rear of the chapel, and the folding chairs which usually faced forward in straight, tight rows were reversed and placed in a rather loose semicircle around the old rock hearth, leaving a large open area just in front of the fireplace for the performers to stand.

The concert grand would be situated just off-center. Several large throw rugs were laid here and there, with some antique floor lamps giving off their soft light. The glow of the fire was the crowning touch to a very lovely parlor setting for an old-fashioned recital. Dark suits and dresses were a must for all in attendance, while the performers were attired in tuxedos and formal gowns. It really was lovely, but some of us did not attend. We had other plans for the concert. . . .

At this point, it is necessary for me to direct your attention to the property adjacent to the campus at the foot of a ravine. There, across the fence, was a chicken coop serving as permanent residence for a half-dozen fat Rhode Island Reds, one of which was surprised to find herself stuffed into a gunnysack. Then I waited on the roof of the chapel, keeping vigil next to the chimney on the upwind side.

The recital was going well, and the audience sat in rapt attention as the artists presented the fruit of their labors. First there was a vocal rendition, then a keyboard selection, and next a duet from an oratorio in Latin or some other foreign tongue. Finally, the fire had died down and the last performer had taken his classic stance, with hands folded chest-high. The accompanist struck up the familiar introduction of "The Holy City," and the singer's bow tie fluttered on his Adam's apple in preparation for his entrance.

We all know that timing is everything, and the right time had just about arrived. Here came the last eight bars: "Hosanna in the *high-est*. . . ." And here came the chicken down the chimney and into the fireplace, flapping and squawking, ashes flying. The recital is over—and what a finale!

On a number of occasions I convinced the dean that my errant ways were caused by frustration, when actually they were prompted by just plain orneriness. However, one nocturnal escapade was more the result of hunger than of either frustration or orneriness.

During my first few months at college, my roommate (an upperclass-man) and I shared an upstairs room in the short wing just off the kitchen. Inevitably, I found a crawl space in the attic that led over to a trap door directly above the kitchen. Just where in the kitchen ceiling it came through I could not tell at first, because the room was pitch-black as I opened the trap door and peered in, but I aimed to find out. So the first night I just lay there in the dark with my head stuck through the trap door, enjoying the smells. You'd be surprised at how good a kitchen smells when you can't do anything but smell it!

I guess my roommate must have missed me shortly before midnight. At any rate, the shaft of light coming from the Dutch door off the hallway, which I had left ajar, suddenly widened out to frame a tousled head of hair. A voice said, "Who is that?"

It was a partial relief to recognize my roommate's voice. I answered, "It's me."

He said, "What are you doing?"

I said, "I'm praying, and I didn't want to disturb you." He went back to bed, and I kept on smelling. But pretty soon I did pray a little bit. The kitchen smells reminded me just how far from home I was (as well as making me hungry), and I was feeling lonesome, scared, and frustrated. I knew that God could help me if I would let him. But that was a big "if."

The next morning, after breakfast, I hung around the dining room talking to the students who had "kitchen duty" (serving tables) that week. I found one little gal who was feeling a little sick, and I offered to "sub" for her at lunchtime. I had never had kitchen duty before, so we had to go to the hostess to get me approved. Well, the hostess thought I was very gallant to offer. They both shook my hand, and we all felt good about the situation. But I was the one who felt the best.

I showed up for lunch fifteen minutes early and put on my apron in the anteroom that connected the dining hall to the kitchen. I couldn't wait to get into that kitchen, but I didn't want to appear anxious. Finally, the cook swung the double doors open and said, "You can start now." I entered the inner sanctum.

It was sort of a gastronomic holy of holies. Long counters with steaming bowls of gravy, bowls of mashed potatoes piled up like white mountains, colorful bowls of mixed vegetables, and platters of Spam®—which, you may know, is similar to meat but not quite the same. It is very salty and can give you a heartburn. But it sure was good at the time.

For a moment I almost forgot my mission—looking for that trap door. But then my eyes swept the ceiling, and my heart sank. It was snow-white with an enameled finish and not a trap door in sight. How could I have so grossly miscalculated? And then I was moving away, headed for the dining hall with two hot bowls of food. But I had more trips to make—more opportunities to case the kitchen.

The next time I headed the long way around, going behind the counter to the very end and then back around to pick up the platters. Then, about four paces from the end of the counter, I saw it. Not plainly at first; it was just an identation in the ceiling with bullnose corners. It was the same snow-white as the rest of the ceiling, and you had to be right on it to see it, but it was there all right. I had found my trap door.

Before I took off my apron that noon, I had that trap door all lined and sighted. There would be a little problem on the first drop through, especially in a pitch-dark room. It was a pretty high ceiling, and unfortunately the trap door was sort of halfway over the counter and halfway over the floor. I would have to swing a little bit one way and land on the counter or a little bit the other way and land on the floor; I'd be in big trouble if I didn't swing at all! A quick glance back for one last lay of the land registered some large crocks and five-gallon metal containers nearby filled with who-knows-what. But I figured they would be cleared away before the day was over.

About midnight I decided to go to the attic to pray. The trap door opened easily, although it seemed to creak more loudly on its hinges than it had before. I swung my legs through the opening and sat there in the silent blackness. I felt as if I were sitting on the rim of a giant inkwell getting ready to jump.

In my mind, I went over the distances, the surfaces, and the placement of the objects in the room. Being able to see a little bit—even just a shadowy reflection from a surface to give me some perception—would have helped. But I could see nothing but blackness.

The longer I waited the smarter I got, so I decided to jump while I was still dumb enough. I slid down until just my elbows were hooked over the sides. Wow! That hurt. The pain blotted out my careful plans of swinging one way or the other. My arms just gave way, leaving some hide in the process, and down I plummeted.

I ended up on the floor after bouncing off the counter, and I hurt in several places. I also found out what was in one of those big crocks. It was lard, and I was in it up to my elbow.

I felt my way to the back door, undid the safety latch, let myself out, and spent the next half-hour cleaning lard off my arm. Then I went back to bed—my stomach still empty.

The next day, not a thing was said about the noise or the mess. So I acquired a pencil flashlight and made several successful raids. Then one night I discovered a padlock through the latch of my trap door, and I never went to the attic to pray again.

My college years were also war years, and gas rationing was hitting everyone pretty hard about that time. Transportation became a real problem. But I had the answer. I bought a 1930 Harley Davidson motorcycle with a suicide clutch. Could that critter ever go far and fast on a gallon of gas!

One Sunday morning my roommate, Kay, said, "Let's go to the store and buy some grub." (We had both slept through breakfast, and the noon meal on Sunday was usually not served until one-thirty or two. We headed out the back door of the men's lower dormitory, climbed aboard the old Harley, and jetted down Avenue 64 toward the Highland Park Food Mart, shattering the Sunday stillness of old Pasadena.

The menu was really sort of biblical—a loaf of bakery bread, a wedge of Swiss cheese, and a bottle of grape juice. At the last minute, we switched the grape juice to a bottle of cheap wine, which turned out to be the sorriest substitution I've ever made. I had managed to get clear through high school without even a taste of beer. And now, on a Sunday morning, sitting in the dorm at Bible college, I was washing down bread and cheese with water glasses full of red wine. I got warm and dizzy. Then one of my neighbors down the hall asked me to trim his hair for church. I'm afraid I nearly butchered him.

The next day, both my roommate and I were called into the president's office. The dean of men was there, too. It really looked bad. Before we went in, we tried to get our story straight. My roommate said, "Now remember, we had kept a jug of apple juice below the sink in the room, and it must have fermented."

They called me in first, and after some awkward preliminaries, I said, "Would you believe me if I told you we had some apple juice that had fermented?"

They said, "No, unless it was red apple juice." Obviously they had an eyewitness, and I would bet he had a funny-looking haircut.

At any rate, I said, "OK, I'm guilty, where do we go from here?" They said that, because of the seriousness of the case, they would take it up with the faculty and let me know.

The result of that escapade was that Kay and I were both "campused" for one whole semester, which means just what it sounds like—we were stuck on campus. If we needed a haircut or an appendectomy, the dean would take us there. Otherwise, we could go to meals, classes, chapel, prayer meetings, the shower, and bed—period. My music projects slacked off to practically zilch. Nobody wanted to sing with a winebibber. And I had to refuse all invitations for personal appearances, although of course I didn't give the real reason. I'd just say, "My calendar is full, thank you."

The worst part was that, after the "sentence" was handed down, the dean "let" me go home to talk it over with Dad and Mom. I was sorry for what I had done, and I was pretty sure I could count on God to forgive me. But I wasn't too sure about the folks. That was a long trip home, but I was wrong about my parents. Not only did they forgive me, but Dad let me decide if I wanted to go back and face the music or change schools for a new start. Well, I had made a lot of dumb decisions before, and I would make many more in years to come, but at least I made a right one that day. I said, "Dad, I'm going back and take my punishment."

I probably got more book-learning done during the semester I was campused than in all of the other semesters combined. That doesn't mean I earned any halos during that period, because I'd get pretty angry at times being stuck there by myself. And Kay was no help; we just never communicated much after that.

I remember one Sunday afternoon when I got a bad case of the "poor me"s. It was a holiday weekend, and the campus was really deserted. There was to be no "sit-down" evening meal, and for the half-dozen students still on campus they were going to serve sandwiches and milk in the pantry at half-past six. My studies were pretty well caught up, and I had practiced the violin for three hours. Let's face it—I was bored and spoiling for trouble. And I found it in the form of a fiendish scheme.

Ambling into the dining room, I took careful note that not a soul was in sight. The peaceful, simple elegance of the room was a perfect backdrop against which to make a rebellious statement. The hardwood floors were highly polished; the white-linen-covered tables were in perfect formation, each one lovingly adorned with glassware, china, and silverware (not sterling); the salt and pepper shakers were freshly filled and wiped free of fingerprints; the sugar bowls were freshly half-filled. (We were in the middle of that bothersome thing called sugar rationing.) The French doors and windows, with their frilly white curtains, filtered the rays of the afternoon sun, and just standing there was almost a spiritual experience. What a contrast to the melee that would break loose about ten minutes into breakfast on Monday morning!

I quietly made the rounds, pausing briefly at each table for a quick twist of the wrist, and within five minutes the dirty work was done. I laughed till I cried, conjuring up visions of what would take place the next morning.

To fill you in on our breakfast ritual, it went something like this: Everyone would file in at exactly seven in the morning and, moving to an assigned table, would stand behind his or her respective chair. No one sat, yet. At the head of each table was a faculty member. When everyone was in place, the hostess, who was at the head of the center table, would rap on her glass with a knife handle and call on whomever she pleased to return thanks. Then everyone would be seated.

Next, the waiters (the students on kitchen duty) would glide through swinging doors with bowls of hot oatmeal, and since there was a waiter for each table of ten, everyone was served within about fifteen seconds. Next, the head of each table would lift the lid from the sugar bowl, plop in a spoon, and pass the bowl to the right. When it returned to the head of the table, the faculty member would then take a spoonful. Meanwhile, the pitcher of milk would likewise make the rounds. Finally, the head of the table would pick up a tablespoon and, holding it at the ready, proceed to take the first bite. That was the signal for the whole table to dive in.

On the particular Monday morning in question, I slept in. There was nothing unusual about that, but it was especially necessary this Monday. Actually, I didn't exactly *sleep* in; I just *lay* in . . . and waited. Sure enough, at ten after seven I heard everyone thundering down the stairs, making haste for the latrine. I stuck my head out the door and hollered, "What's going on?" A voice wheezed back, "You should have been there; somebody salted the sugar bowls!"

The shock waves of that stupid little prank produced two effects— one negative and the other decidedly positive. The bad news was that on Tuesday morning at chapel they announced that butter would be taken off the tables until the culprit confessed. The good news was that, starting that very Monday in chapel, a special silent prayer time was observed for soul-searching. As everyone sat with bowed head, the dean recited the story of Achan with "sin in the camp" and encouraged the Achan of Southern California Bible College to step forward. Nobody did.

On Tuesday after the "no butter" announcement, there was another long period of silent prayer, which ended up not so silent because students started confessing more to God than "sugar bowl" violations. By Friday it looked as if we might be headed for a full-blown revival. Sure enough, when chapel convened the following Monday, the spirit of confession and travail picked up where it left off on Friday and continued through the week, gaining momentum as the days went by. On Wednesday, chapel ran into the first regularly scheduled class period, and on Friday chapel lasted until lunchtime. Practically everybody in school confessed something, although nobody ever confessed to putting the salt in the sugar bowl. The following Monday, butter quietly reappeared on the tables, and the campus returned to normal.

I've heard of sound sleepers, but there was one student on campus who was truly remarkable. I was skeptical when this heavy sleeper's roommate said he (the sleeper) had agreed to make the roommate's bed every morning in exchange for being awakened on time each morning. And that was no easy task, I was told; it included face slaps, cold water, name-calling, and on occasion a zombie-like waltz around the room.

I finally got a chance to verify the story, however. Shortly after dinner on a Tuesday night, I answered a rap on the door. It was the sleeper's roommate. He said that he was needed at home for a day due to illness in the family, and asked if I would please awaken the sleeper the next morning.

I agreed, and then I started thinking. I thought about how shy the sleeper was, and how easily he was embarrassed. Then I wondered if he really did sleep all that soundly or if he just liked the attention his reputation brought him. Guardedly, I shared these concerns with several other students up and down the hall, and by the time I slid into bed I was so excited I couldn't sleep. Twice during the night, I crept down the hall to the sleeper's room to check on him, thinking how unfortunate it would be if insomnia struck him awake that night. But each time I looked in, he was doing fine.

When the alarm went off at six-thirty the next morning, I hit the deck and started getting ready for breakfast. I knew my little group of cohorts would be doing the same. On the way up the hall I looked in on the sleeper, and he was still doing fine—nice, long, steady breathing; then an occasional sharp intake that would collapse a nostril and cause him to snort. Everything was in order.

Standing in line, waiting to enter the dining hall, I gave our little group the good report, and we synchronized our watches; we were to make our move at exactly seven twenty-five. Out of the six of us, all but two sat at different tables. Two at one table was awkward but couldn't be helped.

The oatmeal came. And then we waited: the eggs . . . where were the eggs? It appeared our table would have to wait for its eggs, even though all the other tables had theirs. I glanced down at my watch: seven twenty-one. The eggs might still make it. At exactly seven twenty-four our waiter came smiling up to our table as if he had just invented eggs fried in bacon grease. At seven twenty-five the platter was directly in front of me, but I had to leave right then. I bequeathed my cackleberries to the girl across from me and hurriedly begged to be excused. We had just five minutes to do what we had planned.

When we all arrived at the sleeper's room, we entered and stepped across to his bed. As carefully as possible, we lifted the mattress off the springs and moved it out over the edge of the bunk. Then we paused to see what would happen. The sleeper didn't stir. In the next move he was airborne, and like pallbearers carrying a mattress casket we were on our way—down the hall, out the front door, across the broad expanse of campus lawn, over the asphalt drive, down the hill, through the quad, and right up on the front porch of the girls' dormitory. Still the sleeper slept, even when we yanked off the covers and revealed his striped pajamas.

We fled back the way we had come, and on the way we picked up the dignified strains of the Doxology, which was always sung at breakfast and after which everyone was formally dismissed. Now the fun was about to begin.

We ran through the lower hallway of the men's dorm, cut through the administration building, and came out in front of the chapel to mingle with the other students. Most of the female population would then migrate towards the girls' dormitory before returning to chapel. Looking back, we had a clear view of our handiwork, and our sleeper looked like a giant Christmas package left on somebody's front porch.

Shortly there commenced a wave of giggling and screaming, whooping and hollering. Somebody must have pushed the right button, for suddenly out of the crowd of young ladies on the porch bolted a lone striped figure, clutching a pillow. His movements were sporadic and jerky; he was barefoot, and covering the distance between the two dorms was like crossing a mine field. There were pebbles on the cement, rocks on the asphalt, thorns in the flower beds, and twigs on the lawn.

When our sleeper (awake at last) hit the door of the men's dorm, we broke into a chorus of the old Gypsy Smith favorite, "Let Me Dream On If I Am Dreaming," and that became his theme song ever after. Oh, he was mad. The problem was he wasn't real sure whom to be mad at.

I reasoned with him, saying, "The experience you just had is an answer to a shy man's prayer. For about three minutes, there you were, the most popular man on campus." And I left him meditating on that with a grin on his face.

I hope there will be crowns all around for my professors, the president of the college, the dean, the hostess, and the counselors. I'll tell you, they were longsuffering saints—every one of them.

They all looked upon that first year in school as my "adjustment period," as they called it. My home life had been pretty closely supervised. My folks' presence had been sort of like a giant thumb that had me squashed down like a coiled spring. When I slipped out from under that thumb and went off to college, I just flipped and bounced all over the place. And if anybody ever needed adjusting, I guess it was me. Thank God most of the kids who arrive at college are already in some state of adjustment or it would really be a crazy farm.

I'm glad to leave out a lot of things that happened that year, because there is no point in opening old wounds, but before I really got adjusted I still had some things to get out of my system. For example, at one point I took to sliding down the rainpipe from our dormitory window about an hour after lights-out and coasting the Harley Davidson down the alley to the back street. Then I'd switch on the ignition and headlight, put her in gear, let out the clutch, and blast off. I'd take long rides—I mean for hours. Sometimes I'd just barely beat the sun back to the campus. I'd hit the foot of the hill at just the right speed and cut the ignition and headlight. Then I would coast up the alley like a big black cat, make a half-turn, and come to rest between two gigantic eucalyptus trees. I'd crawl back up the drainpipe, through the window, and under the covers.

I never once got caught at these nightly escapades, but my roommate did. Just one time he took his girlfriend to a supper club. Afterwards, in a seizure of guilt, she told somebody, and it got back to the dean and faculty. That was that. Mr. Roommate was a fifth-year student about one semester away from his Th.B., but he was expelled and never came back. The last I heard he was driving a moving van. I still do not know why it was him and not me. But I am sure that seeing what happened to him put me a long way down the road to total and permanent adjustment!

six

SHAKING HANDS WITH GOD

Looking back, as I often do, I can see without a doubt that during my college years God had His hand—and occasionally, even His fist—on me all the time. With my probation period behind, I looked forward to the things that lay ahead.

I was free to accept invitations to play the violin again. So, with a team of singers and a marvelous student pianist named Millie Vale, each Wednesday evening I would go down on Main Street to a little dingy storefront church called Christ Faith Mission. It was great to see the derelicts respond to the music and the message. Not all of them were drunks; some were just young guys down on their luck, having landed in Los Angeles from some faraway place, broke and lonely.

I recall that during the rides down to the mission in the school station wagon I always felt uncertain and a bit apprehensive about what I would encounter, but going home I always felt warm and glowing all over. Going in, I would feel so empty and helpless, as though I had not a thing to give—because I really didn't. But we would just give them Christ—His love, mercy, strength, and grace—and they would respond to Him. That's when I first began to contemplate grace and the apparent struggle or contradiction between mercy and justice. But I also learned firsthand just how powerful grace is; we were seeing it at work.

Another thing that stands out in my memory is a touring choir that Marcus Gaston got together to take a little public-relations trip up the coast during one Easter vacation. I went to rehearsal and signed up. Rev. Gaston was probably the youngest member of the faculty, and he was also one of the greatest guys you'll ever meet. What an inspiration he was to me! About the third night out he said to me, "Why don't you conduct one of the numbers?" I had led congregational singing before, but not an honest-to-goodness choir! I found out that I liked conducting.

In 1946 Bob Bowman gave up his position as choirmaster of Calvary Assembly in Inglewood, California, to work full time with a radio missionary organization called The Far East Broadcasting Company. I had been to his church on a number of occasions to play the violin, and I considered it one of the best in Southern California. Now, I'm not sure how this all came about, but I was thrilled beyond words when Pastor William J. Roberts offered me Bob's old job on a trial basis. He really stuck his neck out a mile, because the sum total of my choir experience at that point was having conducted the school choir that one time for Marcus Gaston. Nevertheless, I jumped at the chance.

One of the duties that went with the job was writing a new choir arrangement each week. Imagine getting paid for arranging—I couldn't believe it! Pastor Roberts also did a radio program, *The Family Bible Hour,* each afternoon from the old KFWB studios in Hollywood, and three times a week I played a violin solo on this program. From the college campus to Inglewood and Hollywood was a long way, and those days it seemed I spent half my life driving. But I was doing what I liked.

I really have to take a moment here to tell you about Bob Bowman. He's a "true blue" person. Besides helping me find my way around in my new position as choir director, he gave me my first job arranging for instruments. He was getting ready to record an album of vocal solos and duets and thought it would be nice to add some strings in the background. Would I like to do the writing? he asked. I figured if I were going to be a real arranger, I ought to know how to write for strings, and this was as good a place as any to start. I used two violins, one cello, one harp, and keyboard. I don't remember what I wrote, only that it was the first time I wrote for strings.

While I was busy working at the Inglewood Church, the pace on campus was quickening as well. I now had organized an eight-piece brass choir—four trumpets and four trombones. This meant more writing and more rehearsing. It was during this time that I began to burn the midnight oil on a regular basis.

I was also in the process of talking Rev. Roberts and the church elders into some more staff additions. I had met a talented Scandinavian kid who could really play the piano, and I talked him into joining us in our music endeavors in Inglewood, even though he was still in high school in Pasadena. His name was Charlie Magnuson.

Eventually, I also got Linnie and John Olson to move to Inglewood. Then we added a harp player. (We even bought a harp!) The church board was appalled at the money I was spending, but they could see that the people were enjoying the music, so they agreed to what I asked. So now I had Linnie at the organ, Charlie at the piano, and Bill Becker at the harp, with every seat in the choir full.

Bob Bowman would pay occasional visits to see how things were going, and he taught me many lessons. For example, during a break in a rehearsal, he took me aside and said, "When you conduct a choir, it's not the same as leading congregational singing."

You see, I have arms that hang down to my kneecaps with a wingspan of exactly six feet, six inches when fully extended. When I got to flailing away like a wounded helicopter, I could be downright distracting for the congregation as well as the choir. So dear Bob tried to tell me as gently as possible that perhaps I could get the job done better if I were less demonstrative. It was good advice, and I've had occasion to review it through the years.

Another time I had invited my eight-piece brass choir to perform on the broadcast. It was a special occasion of sorts, and Bob Bowman was also on the program. I had written some fancy arrangements for the program and kept urging everybody to sing and play more loudly. I wanted more, more, more.

After the broadcast, some of the ladies served coffee and donuts for the entire staff and guests. Bob took me into the kitchen and said, "Let me show you something." He put a small, empty paper cup in my hand and then from the cupboard produced a huge glass pitcher. Motioning me to the sink, he filled the pitcher to the brim with water, then turned it upside down over my little cup. Water splashed everywhere, including on my shirt cuff. With a grimace I searched his expressionless face for an explanation.

Finally he said, "How much water did you get out of that pitcher of water?" The obvious answer was "Less than a cupful." He said, "Well, remember, those microphones are just like that cup. You might throw buckets of sound at them, but they are only taking cupfuls." That day started my pilgrimage to find out how to produce sound as you really hear it. I guess I'll keep trying as long as I live.

In 1947, Bob Bowman and John Broger began producing a weekly radio program for the Far East Broadcasting Company (FEBC). The program was called *The Call of the Orient,* and they asked me to write the music for it. It was an innovative format that included a missionary story underscored with orchestral bridges and cues. I'd never written a cue in my life, but I got together an oboe, a flute, a harp, and some strings and started to learn. We recorded each week out in Santa Monica at the Moody Institute of Science on their large soundstage. One of the Moody staff members was in charge of recording. His name was Dick Ross, but that's another chapter. . . .

There are several things that stand out in my memory from the time I was doing *Family Bible Hour* broadcast with Rev. Roberts on KFWB. Each day after we went off the air, a western music show would come on. The cowboy band, in boots and loud shirts, would be milling around in the hall and rehearsing off and on while we were on the air. They all talked loudly and roughly, but the main guy was a real tyrant, and I'd always try to stay out of his way. His name was Stuart Hamblen. Little did I know that years later I'd record for him and not be at all afraid.

Another thing I remember was that Thursday was my favorite day at KFWB. A big Armed Forces music show called *Sound Off* was produced on that day. The conductor was Mark Worneau. I remember the first time I discovered the show. I had stepped out the door of our studio complex to go to the parking lot, and very faintly I heard the sound of a big band. The sound would come and go; I'd walk one direction and lose it altogether, then cut back the other way and pick it up again.

I kept looking until I found the building. Occasionally someone would come out of that building, and before the door swung shut I'd get a really good blast of sound. Then again it would be muffled and all but inaudible.

I started circling the building. At the opposite end, by standing right up against the wall, I could feel the vibration of a rhythm section and once in a while hear the crack of a brass fill. At the rear of the building, I walked up a ramp and saw a large sliding door marked "Stage Entrance." It was open about a foot, so I slipped inside and stood in the shadows. I couldn't see what was happening on stage, but I could hear much better. It was all there—the brass, the saxes, the strings, and a rich-sounding male choir. Then once in a while, instead of saxes, I could hear woodwinds, and the whole thing was pushed along by the rhythm section.

I had heard a couple of road bands and listened a lot to records and radio, but I had never heard anything like this! The strings were as smooth as butter and seemed to ooze through all the cracks and empty spaces left by the horns. I was transfixed. My heart beat faster, and my palms began to feel clammy. I had my violin case under my arm, so people coming and going never gave me a second glance.

I stayed right there until the rehearsal broke up. But as the musicians began filing offstage, I lit out of there and headed back to the parking lot, almost resenting my one little fiddle. It seemed so weak and useless, like a BB gun fired at an elephant.

On the way home that day, I talked to God about a couple of things. My prayer was mostly inaudible, but once in a while I'd speak right out loud. The gist of the conversation was that there had to be a way to use the sounds I had just heard to proclaim the gospel. Why not? All melody, harmony, pitch, and rhythm belonged to Him. Instead of using lyrics about "people love" and "people things," I could use lyrics about "God love" and "God things."

Then, like most of us have done at one time or another, I made a deal with God: If He would help me with this project, He could have complete ownership of it. Furthermore, I'd agree to a lifetime contract; that is, no matter what happened or how long it took, I'd never quit trying.

That was it. Just as sure as I ever shook hands on a deal, I shook hands with God that day.

The following Thursday, after I played my little solo on the *Family Bible Hour* broadcast, I was back again at the studio on the northwest corner of the KFWB lot for the last hour of the *Sound Off* show. Only this time I walked right in the front door and sat in the back of the auditorium where the studio audience would be sitting in a couple of hours. I just let them play the whole dress rehearsal for me, an audience of one. I counted every man in every section—I remember their positions and numbers to this very day. My brain was tabulating and storing faster than an IBM computer.

About a mile further west on Sunset Boulevard were two giant studio complexes. The first was CBS. Then a couple of blocks down, at the corner of Sunset and Vine, was NBC. On Tuesday after our broadcast, I headed down the street to take a look around. It wasn't long before I had some more bands to listen to. Both NBC and CBS had staff orchestras in those days, and they were producing some magnificent live radio—especially *The Bekins Hour,* starring Lucille Norman singing in front of a large orchestra conducted by Lud Gluskin, and *Hit Parade,* starring Frank Sinatra with the Axel Stordahl Orchestra and the Ken Lane Singers.

I listened. Oh, did I ever listen. While I was a steadfast believer in miracles, it seemed to me that a more logical approach to accomplishing what I was dreaming of would be to assemble some of the ingredients this miracle was going to take. My idea was to get them side by side to make God's work a little easier, you might say.

Back on campus I quietly started sleuthing. I already had the trumpets and trombones. But now, between classes and during lunch hour, I started talking to everyone, asking if they or anyone they knew had played a saxophone or clarinet in high school. I also needed a string bass, a guitar, and a drummer. I quizzed every new student who enrolled.

Can you imagine the trouble I had trying to get an aspiring minister to play a baritone saxophone? We didn't even have one at the school; I had to rent a second-hand instrument with my own money from Lockie Music Exchange on South Broadway in downtown Los Angeles. It was too beat-up to sell, so the proprietor let me rent it for eight dollars per month.

I still remember the guy who finally agreed to try to play the thing; David Champion was his name. He had played an alto sax in high school, but had never played a note on the baritone. The day I brought that hunk of plumbing on campus, it caused quite a commotion. David met me at the door, and we whisked the mysterious-looking monster through the hall and down to a seldom-used classroom in the basement.

By the time he got it hooked together, we had quite a group of spectators. Then came the moment of truth. Would he be able to play it? David puffed up and got red in the face, and out came a honk like an air horn on an eighteen-wheeler. But we finally had our baritone sax, which rounded out the section; two altos, two tenors, and a baritone.

It took several months to assemble the personnel for our "big band," but the day finally came for our first full-blown rehearsal. I had two arrangements ready to go. Bob Shephard, who was one of my best buddies in college (and just as poor a student as I), had helped me copy the arrangements, and he also played lead trombone in the band. We had stayed up most of the previous night in preparation for—and in anticipation of—that first rehearsal.

What a sight it was—four trumpets standing across the back, four trombones seated in front of them, and the five saxophones on the front row. The bass, guitar, piano, and drums were to my left. It was wall-to-wall band, and I had to stand in the doorway to conduct, while the curiosity seekers jammed the hallway. And it just so happened that this classroom was directly below the administration office, as well as the office of the president and a large faculty conference room.

Now, when you detonate a seventeen-piece stage band, it may be good or it may be bad, but in either case it's loud. It wasn't long until a messenger was dispatched from the offices above to find the cause of all the racket and put a stop to it. Our first rehearsal was very brief, but we rescheduled another for the next day in the gymnasium.

At separate rehearsals I was putting together a sixteen-voice chorus, and finally the day came to combine the band and the chorus. What a time we had! Soon we had built a repertoire of arrangements sufficient to present one full program. The only problem was, we didn't have any invitations to perform.

Finally, they let us play and sing in chapel. But even after that, bookings were slow at first, because this kind of music was controversial—to say the least—in Bible college circles. To say that not everybody liked us is a gross understatement. The school music department was incensed that we would appear in public using the school name, and many churches just plain turned down our offer to appear, even for free.

We had occasional internal problems as well. It seemed that each time we had a wave of spiritual fervor on campus, various members of the band and chorus would "turn from their wicked ways" to spend more time on the sobering pursuits of ministerial preparation, leaving me with vacancies to fill.

In spite of all the problems and setbacks, however, it wasn't long until everyone knew we were serious about our music. There was dedication and discipline. Our rehearsals were preceded with prayer time, and we asked the Lord to mold us into the kind of unit that would be effective in reaching young people with the gospel.

One day a wonderful lady came to our assistance in matters of public relations as well as finance. She was no other than the college president's wife, Mrs. Edna Harrison. In no time at all, there were funds available for instruments, lighted stands, uniforms, and risers. Invitations started pouring in to play at some rather important gatherings, and we even toured up and down the West Coast in the interest of student recruitment.

Between my choir job at Inglewood, the afternoon broadcasts, the weekly program for FEBC, and the college band, my studies really suffered. I flunked both Greek and Hebrew. And not only was I behind in my studies; I was also behind on my school bill. By coincidence, my uncle, Dr. George Carmichael, had been dean of men during the previous year. That hadn't hurt one bit. Occasionally he had cautioned me about scholastics, but as often as not he had also run interference for me. But, when the new dean took over, it was a different story. He wanted less performing and more conforming.

Then, to further complicate matters, I heard a young lady sing. Her name was Evangeline Otto, and she was featured on a late-night broadcast every Sunday. After listening for several weeks, I decided I should meet her. I finally arranged it, and not only could she sing, but she was also beautiful and seemed to like me. She was attending Bible school at Angelus Temple and was one of the staff soloists. She was also singing regularly in the Wilbur Nelson Trio, which was an exceptional group heard daily on radio. We shared many common interests, not the least of which was music. After a few weeks I talked her into coming out to my church to sing. And that's not the only thing she agreed to. We were married shortly thereafter.

Vangie (Evangeline) and I figured it would be best to use a neutral location for the ceremony—her church was too large, mine too small. So, on a balmy Sunday afternoon in 1948, in the main auditorium of old Bethel Temple in Los Angeles, we tied the knot and became Mr. and Mrs. Between her circle of friends and my circle of friends, we had quite a crowd. I had thought about having the band play, but regained my reason at the last minute and settled for something a bit more modest. Mom and Dad drove down from San Jose, and Dad performed the ceremony.

On the way out, amid hurled rice and exploding flash bulbs, I spotted Dr. Harrison (the college president) and, leaning in close, negotiated the loan of a twenty-dollar bill. Vangie and I had a very spartan honeymoon. Then, with my domestic affairs in order and two mouths to feed instead of one, I plunged back into my work with a vengeance.

seven

MOVING OUT

One of the really great gifts that God has given to me throughout my life is people and their friendship. I've learned from them, I've learned on them, I've learned with them.

One of those special friends to me was Earle Williams, whom I met during my last year at Southern California Bible College. Earle had just started a company called Sacred Records. He gave me my first opportunity to record a violin solo album, which I did with Loren Whitney at the pipe organ. And over the coming decade he would give me the chance to experiment with new kinds of gospel music even though he would be criticized for it and almost go broke financing it.

Meanwhile, back on campus, graduation time was approaching. My last year of college had been a blur of music and activity, but I managed (barely) to scrape together enough money to stay in school, but Hebrew and homiletics were a disaster.

The Pasadena Civic Auditorium was reserved for the graduation exercises. It was decided that we would turn the whole student body into a choir for this very special night. I got busy and wrote some arrangements for the whole group, and we even brought in my harpist from Inglewood, plus Linnie Olson and Chuck Magnuson. I rented two tympani, tuned them to F and C, and showed a guy how to do a roll, beginning with a forte piano and then building to a crescendo.

That stage on graduation night could not have held another body. With the huge choir singing and the band playing, the harp "glissing" and the tympany thundering, the program sounded like an MGM epic film score. Finally, after all the music and speeches, the graduating class in caps and gowns started filing across the front of the stage to receive diplomas while the band and organ struck up "Pomp and Circumstance."

The certificates being presented were for the Bachelor of Arts Degree in Theology and were beautifully enclosed in rather ornate, simulated leather folders. I was the last in line to cross the stage. Dr. Harrison flipped the tassel of my cap from one side to the other, shook my hand, gave me a big smile and handed me my folder. That's all I got—just the folder with nothing inside. (Hebrew and homiletics were just too much for me!)

But getting that empty folder didn't hurt too much, because two days earlier I had been offered a position on the faculty to head up a newly formed department. It was called the "department of evangelistic music," and its creation served a dual purpose. The school would have my continued services in those certain areas of music that were growing ever more visible and useful; also, it was agreed that half of my salary was to go toward my delinquent school bills.

A discussion with Dr. and Mrs. Harrison determined that as head of the new department I would work toward two goals: the building of a forty-piece concert band, using the stage band as a nucleus, and the recruitment of a permanent forty-voice choir. I liked the feeling of being legitimatized. After sneaking around doing underground rehearsals for years now, I had been given a badge of approval and was getting paid to boot.

Now that the stage band had broken the ice, you'd be surprised how many clarinets, flutes, cornets, trumpets, trombones, saxophones, baritone horns, and tubas came out of the closet. Some kids had their folks send their instruments from home; some of them retrieved them in person. It wasn't long until the band was in regular rehearsals and growing. I bought all the standard band marches like "Washington Post" and "Stars and Stripes Forever." Soon we were playing at all the conventions and rallies in Southern California.

Meanwhile, the choir prospered as well, and our repertoire was about half published anthems and half original arrangements of mine. When they got suited up in the dark blue robes with gold satin shawl collars, they looked as good as they sounded. (The band also had blue uniforms with gold trim and braid.)

Those were exciting days. As I look back, the good is mostly what I remember. Oh sure, there were disappointments, misunderstandings, hurts, and a lot of hard work. But dreams were coming true and, just as quickly, new dreams were taking their place.

There were three "cause factors" that propelled me on: (1) a natural curiosity about music that kept me experimenting; (2) a gnawing dissatisfaction with the status quo that kept me fighting; and (3) a compulsion to share the gospel that kept my heart open to God's will in my life. And oh, how I depended on those special people in my life such as William J. Roberts, Dr. Harrison, Bob Bowman, John Olson, my buddy Bob Shephard, and my wife, who patiently waited through the long night hours while I put notes on pages.

On more than one occasion, we took long tours up and down the West Coast with the stage band and male choir, and now I had Vangie to sing solos with the band as well. We hit all the big churches and YFC rallies, and even went as far north as Portland and Seattle. Of course, we were not always well received. One time in Oakland, right in the middle of a number, the pastor stepped up to me and said with a scowl, "Stop at the end of this verse." In San Francisco, while unloading the equipment, the custodian at Glad Tidings Temple saw the drums and said, "You're not bringing those things into this church." I finally reached a compromise with the pastor, and we hid the drums behind a drape hanging from a pipe railing in front of the choir loft. But the atmosphere was tense, and we were never invited back.

Back in President Harrison's office after the first tour, I gave him a full account of our wins and losses. The Doc was beautiful. He could hardly carry a tune (I know; I had stood beside him during congregational singing), but he saw possibilities in our crude attempts to use a new kind of music in evangelism. He told me about the criticism he had received when he campaigned to get our college fully accredited. Then he prayed that God would keep our motives pure and our hearts strong.

During that first year as head of the department, I had two appearances scheduled in Pasadena. One turned out to be disastrous; the other was the beginning of something good.

On the campus of Pasadena City College there was a Bible Club that met on a regular basis. Somehow they were given the opportunity to sponsor an assembly. (Such assemblies, in which the entire student body would assemble in the auditorium for some sort of entertainment event, were referred to as "Aud Calls.") Our band was invited to appear on this occasion, and we saw it as a great opportunity to minister. The head of the Bible Club was acquainted with the new-sounding gospel music we were producing and figured it would be just right for the student body; he hoped they'd perk up their ears and listen. Two weeks before we appeared, another big band had been the featured entertainment at an Aud Call—I believe it was Gene Krupa's. But I didn't find this out until later.

At any rate, we got everything set up and ready to go, and the place was packed with a bunch of rowdy college kids waiting to be entertained. Then somebody in front of the big curtain introduced us, and as the curtain went up I kicked the band off. We were nervous, but the first couple of tunes went OK. Then everything started falling apart.

We had decided to use their music stands instead of bringing our own, and their music stands had no lights on them. So when the backstage manager started to get creative with some fancy lighting effects, I saw everybody's head go down into their music stands; they began scuffling for notes. Then about eight bars later, real trouble broke out. I should mention that many of the arrangements had been copied in blue pencil and others in red pencil. So when the electrician threw the blue overhead lights on full blast, the blue notes just plain disappeared from the page. When the red overheads went on, the red notes disappeared. And believe me, we would have liked to disappear as well!

Another Pasadena appearance went considerably better. The band was invited to present the music for the Men's Fellowship at the Mission Covenant Church. We were well received, and everyone enjoyed themselves. Afterwards, a man with a most cordial manner came up and introduced himself as Arnie Peterson and said, "You guys are as good as Spade Cooley and ought to be on TV." (For those of you who don't know, Spade Cooley was sort of a cowboy Lawrence Welk and his was the only music show on TV at the time.)

Arnie continued: "Here's my card. I've written the phone number of the agency that handles my advertising. On Monday, you call a guy by the name of Lou Spruence, and he'll work out the details."

I thought to myself, "Sure, Arnie." On the way home I told Vangie and some of the guys, and we figured at best it was probably a nice form of flattery. But when Monday morning rolled around, I called the number on that card. Before you knew it, old Lou had set up an audition at 1313 North Vine in Hollywood at KHJ-TV (channel 2 at that time).

Before the audition, I made some changes in the group. For versatility, I changed the vocal group to four guys and four gals, and I added nine strings (six violins, two violas, and one cello). After we did our little program for the audition, Arnie and Lou came up on stage and said, "We are going on the air for one program next Tuesday night at eight o'clock. Can you all be back?" We said yes. I had never been on TV in my life. None of us had.

Bright and early the next morning, I broke the outcome of the audition to Dr. Harrison. He appeared happy and troubled at the same time. He pointed out that some mighty fiery Sunday-evening sermons were being aimed at the evils of TV, and it just wouldn't do to have the Southern California Bible College Band on television. The worldly music we were playing was bad enough, but to go on TV would be the last straw. On the other hand, he said (with a grin) that if we were not identified as being from the college, our appearing "just this once" might be "interesting." That was good enough for me, and we decided to call the telecast *The Campus Christian Hour.*

I'll never forget walking down the halls of that gorgeous building with its indirect lighting and highly polished tile floors, the smell of pancake makeup, the exquisitely decorated studios with plush seats and carpets, and the gleaming hardwood stages with lights and cameras and producers and directors. If you think this twenty-two-year-old kid wasn't excited, you're crazy. But I felt something else, too. It was a frightening sense of responsibility mixed with some feelings of uncertainty. But wasn't this what I had asked God for—open doors, the chance to experiment, new opportunities? We had made a deal, and He was keeping His end of the bargain. I knew He expected me to keep mine.

The red light came on, the floor man threw me a cue, and we were on the air. There would be no starting over, no turning back, no "take two"s. This was live TV. You got one chance, and that was it. The band roared. Vangie and the choir sang. I looked into the camera and said a few words about my faith in Christ, and we were "off the air." I was proud of my little group of prospective preachers.

The next day, Arnie and I met with the bigwigs in a conference room around a big oval table. Lou was there, too, doing the talking. When the meeting was over, we had signed a thirteen-week contract.

Dr. Harrison took this latest development back to the faculty, and the word came down that as long as the college name was not mentioned, we could go on the air. We had approval; we had a contract; we had a sponsor (the Folda-Rolla Company, owned by Arnie, which produced baby carriages); and we had a program format. But we didn't have any music; we had used up all we had on the first telecast.

I was still directing the Inglewood choir as well as the college choir, band and other groups, and the only free time I had was between midnight and dawn. So I decided to put those hours to good use. My life would never be the same again.

With the help of two copyists, I set out to feed that music machine with a half-dozen new arrangements a week. My old buddy Bob Shephard, who still played trombone in the band, and Ewald Growl, who played cello in the band, spent tedious hours each week deciphering my miserable manuscripts, transferring the scribbled notes for each instrument onto separate sheets of music paper in more legible form. It was during those days that I came face to face with the sheer panic of fighting to meet a deadline.

In the beginning, we received loads of unfavorable mail about our TV program. In fact, I've always felt that at first the station was interested in keeping us on the air primarily because we were so controversial. But a strange thing started happening by the end of our thirteen-week run. The mail response became overwhelmingly favorable. And as we began building a mailing list, we noticed that many of our early critics had turned out to be our strongest supporters. It was as though people were finally understanding what we were trying to do, and it was working. Kids were tuning in instead of tuning out, and they were hearing a strong Christian witness on television—perhaps for the very first time.

Naturally, our contract was renewed for another thirteen weeks, and then for another and another. Offers and invitations for public appearances started pouring in. I signed a recording contract, and we began producing records of the band and singers. We had many famous guests on the program—people I had never hoped to meet in my lifetime. There were interviews and stacks of press clippings. We even won an Emmy and attended the awards show with our sponsor. The award was presented to us by Earl Warren, who at the time was Governor of California.

The next Monday morning I was called to the president's office. Dr. Harrison said that the board and faculty felt that since the cast of *The Campus Christian Hour* was made up largely of Southern California Bible College students, the school should receive some recognition and credit. The suggestion was made that perhaps the set could be designed to resemble the campus, and reference could be made to the college from time to time. The sponsors didn't go for the idea, but it was gratifying to see that the college now accepted us. I interpreted this as a sign of a change in attitude on the part of evangelicals everywhere.

By the time we had been on the air for seventy-six consecutive weeks, channel 2 had been sold to CBS. The Musicians Union was insisting that my "preacher" band join the union and receive union scale. Many of the cast had to get on with the business of graduation and ordination. So we closed down the show in 1950. It had been a great experience.

In 1951 I got a call from Dick Ross, with whom I had worked on the *Call of the Orient* show at the Moody Institute of Science. Now he was producing a film for Billy Graham called *Mr. Texas,* and he needed a film score. I had already done some music for him with just a handful of musicians on a film called *The Voice of the Deep,* but *Mr. Texas* needed a full orchestra. The fact that I had never done anything like this before didn't seem to bother either of us, so I went full steam ahead on the project.

Scoring the music for one film "doth not a film scorer make," as I soon found out. I had never studied the art in school or ever read a book on the subject. I just wanted so badly to do it that I developed my own system, which at first was quite primitive. Doing background for vocal solos or choral groups was a whole lot different from doing a dramatic film cue. You can't just think in terms of pretty chord changes and melody lines; there is a whole set of musical devices that you must use. Sometimes I'd finish a cue and then check it back on the paino, trying to play the parts for all the instruments, and lo and behold, it would sound like a song. In frustration and disgust, I'd start over.

The total music budget for *Mr. Texas* was eight hundred dollars—and that was to cover musicians, composition, arranging, copying, studio, tape, and sound engineer. The cost of the band alone was twelve hundred dollars! And since they were all union players, the bill had to be paid promptly. The overage came out of my pocket, but it was worth it. Dick Ross had given me the chance of a lifetime to be involved in a brand new kind of gospel music—scoring Christian motion pictures!

Perhaps the best production Vangie and I ever worked on together came about this time—a beautiful, bouncing baby girl named Carol Celeste, who arrived on 30 November 1949. This little bundle brought a new kind of happiness to the Carmichael household, as well as a new kind of responsibility. In the pages to come, I'll try to give a running account of the influence she has had on my life as the years have unfolded.

One day soon after Carol was born, the phone rang. It was Dick Ross again; he was going to give me another chance. Dick said he was producing a film for Dr. Bob Pierce, founder of World Vision, and wanted me to do the score. It was a missionary film called *The Flame.*

Dr. Bob, as everyone called Bob Pierce, was one of the most dynamic men I had ever met. He also loved music. Dr. Bob said to me, "Buddy, you can have whatever you need to do a first-rate job." I took him at his word and went to work writing a score for a forty-piece orchestra and a twenty-voice choir.

I put everything I had into that project, working at it feverishly to the neglect of all my other responsibilities. I found myself shutting out everything and everybody. The worst part about the whole situation was that I was doing it all in the name of dedication.

I wrote all night, every night. Then at daybreak I would sleep a few hours, get up, and grudgingly go about my other duties. I hardly gave a thought to my family; food lost its taste; and the only time I came to life was when I was putting notes on the page again. Preparation for going into the studio to record was the only thing I thought of.

Finally the day came. We had booked the old Radio Recorders Annex on Sycamore Street in Hollywood, which was "the" place to record in those days. I walked into the studio, and Val Valentine, the finest mixer in town, had the studio set up. It was wall-to-wall singers and musicians. My peers in the music business who are reading this will doubt that we had over sixty people in the Annex, but we did.

Something changed in me during that session, and it wasn't all good. Once I had worked with those professional-caliber musicians, I found it hard to be satisfied with my college and church groups.

I remember the feeling of despair that possessed me when I arrived for rehearsal with the college concert band the week after working with the great studio orchestra on *The Flame.* The students were boisterous and noisy. Those who weren't talking loudly were trying to see if they could play high C or better. Some important players were late or absent. But the worst part was that, when we started to rehearse, the band sounded worse than I had remembered. Their sense of pitch and time seemed to have noticeably deteriorated since the last time we had met. The entire rehearsal was like a bad dream to me.

I was feeling similar frustrations with my church choir at Inglewood. In a conversation with two of the professional woodwind players working for *The Flame,* I found that they were also singers and were studying composition at USC. They expressed an interest in the new things that were happening in gospel music, so I invited them to come and sing with us at Inglewood. They showed up for rehearsal on Thursday. One was a tenor, the other was a baritone, and I really appreciated the way they beefed up the male section. But it seemed that I was the only one that did. I could feel an uneasy tension in the air, and very few, if any, of the choir members spoke to them.

Still, the two musicians told me they enjoyed the music and agreed to sing with us in the Sunday morning service. On Sunday I outfitted them in robes. As usual, before the choir filed into the choir loft, I called on one of the members to lead in prayer, and during the prayer I stole a glance at my visitors. Their heads were bowed.

When the music was over and Pastor Roberts stepped to the pulpit to preach, I breathed a little prayer. Wouldn't it be great if those two guys would really listen and respond? I figured we had something they needed, and our choir surely needed them! Afterwards, they shook the pastor's hand and said how much they enjoyed his sermon. Then they asked me if they could come again the following Thursday for rehearsal. I said, "Great," and they left.

About that time, a couple of stalwarts of the choir stepped up and said they wanted a few words with me. The gist of the one-way conversation that followed was that my visitors were not welcome; they were not to come back; and I was not to bring in any more outsiders. I said, "OK," but I wasn't happy about it. Calling those guys and telling them not to come back any more was a hard thing to do.

Since I had experienced the thrill of recording with choirs made up of some of the greatest studio singers in the world, my church choir was also beginning to sound very bad to me. I seldom brought in new arrangements for them anymore, and believe it or not, I was even beginning to dislike the way they looked! My obsession with excellence was making me weird.

Finally, I had a long talk with Rev. Roberts. What a wonderful man he was! He had given me the chance of a lifetime—my first choir job. He had supported my early experiments. He had been patient with my inexperience and put up with my impulsive nature. Now I was letting him down. How could he interpret my actions as anything but downright ungrateful? How could he possibly understand my anger and frustration when I couldn't really understand those feelings myself?

But we talked, and Rev. Roberts understood. We agreed I needed a change of scenery and time to think. So I ended up resigning both my college job and the church choir job. I bought a new car and packed our belongings. Then Vangie, baby Carol, and I headed out on the road.

Left: There is no appropriate caption for this photo. I was only four and too young to fight back. My folks told me that Lord Fauntleroy clothes were "in" and that was that! (Photo circa 1931.)

Above: The Carmichael family portrait: Adele Carmichael (Mom), Richard Carmichael (Dad), Adele, and me (circa 1938). *Below:* Here I am with my college band and male chorus during my junior year at Southern California Bible College, Pasadena (circa 1947).

Left: Evangeline and I accept the Emmy Award for the Campus Christian Hour television program, presented by Governor Earl Warren of California (circa 1950). *Below:* This is one of my favorite pictures. Dr. Billy Graham was my guest on the Campus Christian Hour in 1950. It was our first meeting.

Photo by Sid Avery & Associates

Top: The Baptist Laymen's Hour Singers (circa 1954). *Bottom:* It was a thrill to conduct an 86-piece symphony orchestra during the Tokyo Crusade in the early 1960s.

Left: The Price family portrait. Left to right are Pop Price, Burdette, Mom Price, Frances, Bob, and my darling Marvella (photo circa 1940). *Below:* Mar and I celebrating our first minute of marriage as we leave the wedding chapel at Carmel By the Sea, 28 October 1965.

I might caption this picture "You're in the family now." When I married Mar, I also got three kids and a cat. Left to right are Tiki, Greg, Andrea, and Erin (circa 1965).

My daughter Carol is the best singer in the world. In 1971, a year after this picture was taken, we signed a letter of agreement for recording her first album on the Light Records label.

Photo by Woody Woodward

Over the years it has been my privilege to work with some of the top performers and recording artists of the day—sacred and secular. This page, clockwise from top: Pat Boone (early 1960s), Earl "Fatha" Hines (circa 1962), Roger Williams (circa 1967), and Jimmy Durante (circa 1965).

Photo by Jasper Daily

This page, counterclockwise from top: Nat King Cole (with studio choir in the mid-1960s), Doc Severinson, Kenny Rogers, Debbie Reynolds.

Photo by Jasmine

Top: George Burns was celebrating one of his famous birthdays, an
Hollywood was using the occasion to raise funds for a worthy cause
I was music director for the evening and took the opportunity to mu
with George and some other well-known celebrants. Left to right are Ha
Linden, producer Jimmy Baker, George Burns, yours truly, and Car
Grant (photo circa 1981). *Bottom:* On stage with Ella Fitzgerald an
Mike Douglas—everybody seems to be happy with everybody (circ
1981). *Opposite page:* For 30 years, the recording studios of Hollywoo
were a second home. *Top:* Recording with a large orchestra mean
packing that little room to the limit. *Bottom:* Do you get the feeling th
string section is not really interested in what we're doing

Photo by David J. Pavol

Photo by Woody Woodward

Above: September 24, 1976 was Gospel Music Day in Los Angeles, proclaimed by Mayor Tom Bradley (left) as Andrae Crouch (right) and I look on. *Below:* Cars streamed to the concert in spite of rain that threatened to cancel the event. The Bowl was packed—and the rain let up an hour before the downbeat. *Opposite page:* From the first chord of the overture until the last sounds died away, it was an unforgettable evening.

Back home in the studio. No tuxedo necessary here.

eight

ON THE ROAD AND BACK

We stayed out on the road one solid year. Dr. Bob Pierce at World Vision partially underwrote the tour by having me appear with the film, *The Flame,* which was then newly released. In between those bookings, we scheduled concerts in churches—some large, some small. I wrote letters to every church and YFC rally for which I could find an address. And I made phone calls, lots of phone calls.

During that time I learned a lot of hard lessons about life and about myself. I wish I could tell everyone reading this book that all you have to do is wait for God to teach you one big lesson and then, once you learn it, you're set for life—no more problems; you just close the book and float on through. Well, maybe things work out that way for some people, but they surely didn't for me. The reason I mention this here is that I want it plainly understood that I didn't come back after a year on the road with everything solved. No sir. I came back having learned only what I had the capacity to learn at that time.

For example, I found out that I could appear in public if I had to. But I also found out that I had more music and style to share than I had spirituality and substance. During that year on the road, I constantly examined my own personal faith and became more secure in my commitment to Christ. Furthermore, I came to realize more fully that the whole purpose for my existence was to proclaim the gospel not only through music and the spoken word, but through my life as well. And I became painfully aware that while the music part of me had matured rapidly, the spiritual part of me had been more than somewhat neglected.

There was a recurring comment that was made wherever we went that year: "Please don't talk so much. Sing and play more; that's what people have come to hear." And it occurred to me that maybe I didn't have to preach in order to communicate. Could it be that God was more interested in what I was than what I could do? Perhaps a little more spiritual maturity would make my music more effective. I did a lot of pondering and praying toward that end.

Then, too, I thought back on my recent failures at the college and at Inglewood. Did I really think I was better than the people there because they couldn't play or sing to suit me? No, I really did not think that. And yet I had been so dissatisfied. They had worked hard and done the best they could do. Would God ask for more than their best? It didn't seem likely. And yet maybe their best wasn't my best, and I couldn't bring myself to settle.

Sometimes I would almost have these matters figured out in my head, but my soul was still in deep turmoil. Hadn't I promised God that I would keep trying until Christian music was the best in the world? I just kept traveling and thinking.

It was a hard year, even though in many ways it was fun, too. Sometimes, on the longer hauls, we would have to leave little Carol with Grandma Otto, and those were sad times. For a while, we were fortunate to have the gifted accompanist, Paul Mickelson travel with us. At other times, a former school chum named Norm Sandberg was at the keyboard. We went up and down the West Coast, back through the Midwest, as far east as Florida, and as far south as Texas. And we only got stranded once—but once was enough.

That was the time we checked into the Awahu Hotel in Boise, Idaho. It was Sunday afternoon, and we were to give a concert that evening in a small, local church. I had two dollars plus some change in my pocket, but I was confident that the offering that evening would be sufficient to pay for the hotel, a couple of hot meals, and a tank of gas to get us to the next town.

But it turned out that, even though our appearance at the church had been prearranged and confirmed by mail, the pastor had gone fishing and closed up shop for the month of July. We found this out at half-past seven that night from an old-timer who came around every sundown to sprinkle the crabgrass lawn that was doing its best to stay alive in front of the little white clapboard church. When it came to staying alive, I felt at that moment that the crabgrass had a better chance than I did!

Heading back to the hotel, I tried very hard to like Boise. Come to think of it, there were only two reasons to stay in that town. One was that I didn't have money to check out of the hotel; the other was I didn't have gas to get past the city limits.

Then, as I walked up the steps of that old hotel, my eyes fell on a mighty pretty sight. It was a bright dayglow placard announcing that a special city-wide revival, with Dr. Merv Rosell and his team of singers and musicians, was starting the very next night in the Boise Stadium. Wow! Cy Jackson had to be somewhere around—why, maybe in this very hotel. Cy was the PR man for some very important evangelists and Christian musicians.

Well, Sunday night came and went. Monday night came and went. The hotel bill that I couldn't pay got bigger and bigger, and my gas tank got emptier and emptier. And then Tuesday morning I spotted Cy Jackson in the lobby. Although we had met over in Southern California, I didn't know for sure that he'd remember me. But he did!

"Well Cy, what are you doin' here in Boise?"

"Well Ralph, what are you doin' here in Boise?"

We answered each other's question. Cy answered with the truth, but I told a lie—a big one. I let it be known that Vangie and I had been having some big concerts around the area, and we were pretty glad about having a little breather in our schedule, so we had decided to lay up in the lovely town of Boise and enjoy the food and comforts of the beautiful Awahu Hotel for a few days.

Cy asked if I'd have the time to join Dr. Merv Rosell and himself for a quick bite of breakfast. I glanced at my watch (my stomach growling), and then said I reckoned I could. During breakfast we touched on this and that and I'll tell you, that food tasted mighty good. Then Cy commented on how busy Vangie and I were with concerts and all, and Merv said that was too bad because it would be nice if we could stay over for a few extra days and be part of the music program each night.

Well, I swallowed the mouthful of food I was chewing, took time to wash it down with some black coffee, and, thinking fast but trying to act casual, I countered with the magnanimous offer to check our calendar to see if we could, in fact, stay over and help them out. And I wondered, what did they have in mind financially?

I rushed back and told Vangie to call the front desk and line up a babysitter for Carol: "Just put it on the bill."

The revival was great. We played and sang our hearts out each night and tripped the light fantastic around the stage, leading the singing for the biggest crowd I'd seen in months. We ate regularly and ended the week with enough money to bail out of the Awahu with plenty left over for gas. But, best of all, I had worked for the legendary Cy Jackson.

Years later, I told Cy how broke I had been in Boise. He said, "I sort of figured as much."

One morning while we were touring Texas, I received a message to call Dick Ross in California at once. My heart skipped a beat. There was only one thing I wanted to hear him say when I got him on the phone, and he said it: "Ralph, I sure wish you were in town. I'm doing a sequel to *Mr. Texas* called *Oiltown, U.S.A.,* and I don't know whom to get to do the music."

The following Monday morning I was huddled with Dick Ross over a Moviola machine at Great Commission Films in Sherman Oaks, California, viewing a rough cut of the picture. It was great to be writing again.

For a while after we returned to California, Vangie and Carol stayed with my folks, who were pastoring a church in Ventura. I commuted, picking up the timings for cues in Sherman Oaks, then heading back to Ventura to write. It was a two-hour trip then because there was no freeway, and about one-fourth of it was right along the coastline.

I'll never forget the first time Carol saw the ocean. She was just learning to put words together. Her eyes popped, and she hollered, "Look, daddy—big bath!" Those were happy days for her, and she really had a case on Grandpa Carmichael. He doted on her, and she would entertain him with her shenanigans by the hour.

After several months of this arrangement, we made a practical decision and took a cozy little two-bedroom apartment in Sherman Oaks, just a couple of miles from where Dick was located. We also began attending The Little Church of Sherman Oaks, whose pastor, Rev. Carl Hatch, and his wife were old and dear friends of my folks.

We made a deal. I said I'd play the violin for him occasionally if he'd let me use a piano in one of the Sunday school rooms for my writing at night. So during the day, I'd work with Dick Ross getting the timings for film cues. Then, after dinner, I'd kiss Vangie and Carol goodnight and leave for the church, where I'd spend the night putting notes on the page. Little did I dream that this was the beginning of a pattern that would wreak much havoc and cause much heartache in the years ahead.

After *Oiltown, U.S.A.* there were many other films, such as *London Crusade, Fire on the Heather,The Heart Is A Rebel, Boomerang,* and *Wiretapper.* When I think back on my life in the 1950s, it seems to be one big blur. Things were happening so fast. In addition to the films, I was doing a lot of work with Earle Williams at Sacred Records;

he would record new artists as fast as I could write the arrangements.

My appetite for work during that time was voracious. The more opportunities I got, the more I wanted. I met Hugh Edwards at International Records and started recording for him. I met Bill Brusseau, who had started a film company in Pasadena, and I worked for him. I met Ken Anderson at Gospel Films, and I worked for him.

I was doing much the same thing as far as my church activities were concerned. I had grown up in an atmosphere of denominational isolationism. It had always been implied but not articulated that the Assemblies of God preached the whole truth while every other denomination presented only half the truth; and that, depending on which half they preached, those other denominations might or might not make it to heaven. In fact, my dad had been considered a bit of a liberal because he belonged to the San Jose Ministerial Association, while many preachers in the Assemblies of God would not give the time of day to a minister from another denomination.

Now, since the very nature of my work was driving me farther and farther away from my earlier denominational ties, I felt (or imagined) a sort of disapproval or estrangement from the Assemblies of God. On the other hand, I felt more and more comfortable with my new freedom in the broader circle of interdenominational opportunities. In my youthful arrogance, I had it figured this way: "If you don't like my music, I'll find somebody who does."

So, in those days, I would work for anybody who could afford me, regardless of their denominational affiliation, so long as they named the name of Christ. I didn't care if they sprinkled or immersed; it didn't matter if they spoke in tongues or didn't speak in tongues. As to the question of being premillenial or postmillenial, I wasn't even sure what that *meant*.

One day I received a letter on very impressive-looking stationery. It was signed by "Dr. J. Lester Harnish," who was pastor of Temple Baptist Church in downtown Los Angeles. He said in the letter that he'd like to have lunch with me and asked if I would call his secretary to set it up. The following week we went to lunch, and the week after that I was the new minister of music at Temple Baptist Church.

Dr. Harnish turned out to be one of those super people that God was always bringing into my life at just the right time. He listened to my dreams and then said, "go to it." He would later claim that I brought a new dimension to the ministry of Temple, but the truth is that I got much more than I gave. Dr. Harnish guided and disciplined, motivated and inspired.

Temple Baptist was not an ordinary church. It owned the Philharmonic Building at Fifth and Olive, which was also the home of the Los Angeles Philharmonic Orchestra and the venue for the Los Angeles Light Opera Company. The church offices and educational department were on the fourth floor, along with beautiful Burdette Hall, where we held weeknight services. The Sunday morning and evening services were held in the great Philharmonic Auditorium.

As I set out to perform my duties as minister of music at Temple, I discovered I now had a different attitude toward the people with whom I was working. The choir had the same inadequacies as my previous choirs, but I had developed a new appreciation for the contribution its members made to our music program. And I began to see the ministry of music from a totally different point of view. The work that I was doing with professional singers in the studio was one world, with one set of standards in technical excellence. The work I did at Temple with my volunteer singers was another world, with a different set of standards for technical excellence. I made demands of both groups on the basis of the best that each could give.

I thought of the biblical parable of the widow's mite. A wealthy person might have placed more in the alms box than she had and still not have given his all. But what the widow gave was all she had, and that was very valuable in God's sight. Many times my studio singers and players gave me enough to meet the acceptable level of technical excellence, but it was seldom their personal best. My volunteers at the church almost always gave their absolute best—all they had—and I learned to love them for that. Then, as I learned to express my love to them, they in turn responded. In that atmosphere of freedom, they could give even more and do even better.

Through the years that lesson I learned at Temple has come in mighty handy, for I have worked with hundreds of amateur groups. I am convinced it is essential for a leader to have the sensitivity to know just how far to push a group. It's easy to kill a performance before it ever gets in front of an audience if the confidence and self-esteem of the performers are destroyed in rehearsal. After all, what is the real purpose of a gospel music presentation? Is it to say, "Look what I've done; I've taken this lousy group of singers and made pros out of them"? Or is it to love them for what they are, bring them to their personal best (not the personal best of the group with which I recorded last week), ask God to bless it, then offer it with a pure and happy heart to the congregation on Sunday?

Being on staff at Temple was different from anything I had experienced before. I had a desk and was expected to be sitting at it by nine o'clock in the morning, Monday through Friday. Wednesday evening there was a sit-down dinner prepared in the basement for the staff and church members, followed by the weeknight service in Burdette Hall. This in turn was followed by rehearsals for the music staff, including soloists, quartets, and the choir. It made a long day. I had Saturday off, then came back for two services on Sunday.

I also had to wear a necktie at all times; that was the worst part of the job. And Monday morning after my first Sunday, there was a note waiting for me on the desk when I arrived. I thought I knew what it would say, because all day Sunday the music had been well received, and I felt pretty good about myself. But all the note said was, "Get rid of the argyle socks." It was signed, "J.L.H."

Before starting at Temple, I had told Dr. Harnish about my many outside music activities. He said, "Fine; just don't let anything interfere with your church work." He even let me use the rehearsal hall to write, provided I was current with my church duties. When I was working on a film, I could take certain days off to get my timings, and I would still burn the midnight oil at The Little Church of Sherman Oaks. Night after night I'd turn the lights off at The Little Church of Sherman Oaks at four or five in the morning, silently steal into our apartment, and creep into bed beside Vangie, knowing it would all start over again in two or three hours when the alarm went off.

Dr. Harnish even allowed me to accept an invitation from Roy McKeown to be musical director and emcee for the YFC Saturday Night Jubilee, which was still going strong over at the Church of the Open Door. Roy said, "Let's do something different and special," and we did. I called some of the guys I had been using in the studios on films and recordings and put together a small stage band of six brass, four saxes, and four rhythm. Then we organized a youth choir. At first it was twenty-four voices, but it finally grew to fifty or so.

And then one day while I was at Temple I received a call from Waldo Tucker and Gil Brink, the producers of *The Baptist Laymen's Hour*. They said they wanted to go to lunch. So they met me at the church office and we walked across the street to the Baltimore Tea Room.

The *Laymen's Hour* was one of the highest quality Christian broadcasts on the air. It was sponsored by the American Baptist Convention and was syndicated on stations nationwide. The music consisted of a sixteen-voice male choir accompanied by a grand piano, with solos by John Gustafson, Joe Barclay, and Frank Alpers. The narrator was the famous Art Gilmore, and the speaker was Dr. Frank Kepner.

There was no joking around at that lunch, and I could tell something serious was brewing. I had on my "sincere" suit, so I fit right in with the mood. They finally got around to what was on their minds, which was that they were thinking of offering me a job as conductor on the program. But the accent was on the word, *thinking*. They were concerned about some of the music I had been doing, which they categorized as a bit too "flashy" or "swingy," and they didn't want any razzmatazz on *The Baptist Laymen's Hour*. I wholeheartedly agreed and assured them that I would do just as they directed.

I got the job, and that took care of the only vacancy on my week's calendar—Saturday mornings. I get tired just thinking back over that period in my life!

Life on the Temple staff was never dull. Even the atmosphere and the surroundings provided an air of excitement. Sometimes in the early afternoon I'd take my sandwich, sneak down into the darkened auditorium, and watch Alfred Wallenstein rehearse the Philharmonic. I also remember watching the Light Opera rehearse shows like *Brigadoon, Oklahoma,* and *Most Happy Fella*. And I would dream of the day when we could present the gospel in that musical form. Why not? Each of those musicals had very touching moments when right would prevail over wrong or an expression of human love would be portrayed. And during those moments I'd get a lump in my throat and think how effective it would be to present God's magnificent message of redemptive love in this manner.

Very few churches in those days had what we called "paid quartets," but Temple did. Our quartet was great: soprano Marjorie Webb, alto Barbara Speaks, tenor John Gustafson, and baritone Frank Alpers. They were the section leaders in the choir, and of course would sing any of the solos that appeared in the Sunday morning anthems. On a rotation basis, they would sing featured solos at Sunday morning services as well. Jessie Boals was the pipe organist, and Charlie Magnuson hired on as regular church pianist. Vangie joined forces with Marj Webb and Barbara Speaks to give us a fine women's trio, and Howard Speaks and I teamed up with Gustafson and Alpers to form a pretty fair male quartet. On occasion, we'd put the trio and quartet together for a septet.

One July, Dr. Harnish decided we should do something out of the ordinary for our summer Sunday evening services. (Traditionally, summer attendance slacks off, and some downtown churches even close down in the evenings.) So for four Sunday nights in a row we planned something we called "The Hour of Power." There would be extra advertising and promotion. Our regular choir of forty voices would be expanded to one hundred voices, and special risers would be constructed.

I sold Dr. Harnish on bringing in a ten-piece brass choir, but he sold me on paying for it. Vangie and I had managed to save up six hundred dollars. So I got her to agree to let me draw it out of the bank to pay for the brass choir, with the idea that the arrangements I would write would be so inspiring that Earle Williams at Sacred Records might want to record us and I'd recoup our investment. We called Earle, who said they hadn't had too many calls for brass choir; he'd have to wait and see what we sounded like.

I called the players and got them to agree to play the four Sunday nights in July for five dollars per rehearsal and ten dollars per performance. Figure it out—fifteen dollars per man times ten men times four nights equals six hundred dollars—the total amount of our savings. I'd be broke, but I had my brass choir. These were all union guys, and I was paying less than union scale. I wouldn't dare to try that today! They were top guys, too. I think I remember all their names: The three trumpets were Mannie Stevens, Carlton McBeth, and Whitey Thomas. The three trombones were Lloyd Ulyate, Bob Fitzpatrick, and Johnny Haliburton. The three French horns were Vince DeRosa, Jimmy Decker, and George Price. The tuba player was George Boujoise.

The first night, just before the curtain went up, everyone was milling around trying to find his or her place. I saw this big, craggy-looking guy, with no coat or tie on, who looked sort of lost. I didn't remember having seen his face before, but since I had recruited sixty new bodies to beef up the choir, I didn't think too much about it. I just walked up to him and said, "Tenor or bass?" I was going to tell him where to sit. He turned out to be the renowned choral conductor, Roger Wagner, and he was looking the stage over in preparation for an upcoming concert series!

The Hour of Power was a great success. People attended, and people responded as Dr. Harnish preached and gave the invitations. I never did get that particular six hundred dollars back, although we did record the arrangements we had written, and that led to many more brass choir performances and recordings through the years.

One other thing came out of The Hour of Power. Dr. Harnish asked me to write a little invitation song that the women's trio would step forward to sing at the conclusion of his sermon, while people had their heads bowed. I entitled it, "The Savior Is Waiting."

My first Christmas at Temple, it seemed we should attempt something that had never been done before—at least not by me or at Temple. Dr. Harnish put his resources squarely behind the project, and it developed as follows: We assembled what was promoted as "The All-Baptist Choir," two hundred voices strong, and we went into monthly rehearsals on Handel's *Messiah*. Toward the end, rehearsals were held weekly. I hired about fifty men from the Los Angeles Philharmonic and four of the top oratorio soloists from the Southern California area. My job was to deliver a top-drawer performance of *The Messiah*, while Dr. Harnish's job was to deliver a packed auditorium for the performance. Neither one of us had ever done those particular jobs before.

Actually, the only piece I had ever heard from *The Messiah* was the "Hallelujah Chorus," but nobody knew that except Vangie, and she wasn't talking. I had my secretary check out Sir Thomas Beecham's recording of *The Messiah* from the Los Angeles public library. That was before the days of the LP, so the album consisted of several ten-inch 78s. Dick Ross let me use an old turntable they had in an editing room at Great Commission Films. Hour after hour, night after night, I would stand with my score and conduct an imaginary orchestra, chorus, and soloists while listening to Sir Thomas's recording.

The performance was scheduled for the Sunday before Christmas at three o'clock in the afternoon. The dress rehearsal on Saturday night was like any other—bedlam but fun. Then the big day came. I put on my rental outfit consisting of striped pants, black tails, bow tie, studs, and a cummerbund. I also hitched up my black socks with garters that cut into my calves in a very uncomfortable manner. Dr. Harnish motioned me to the curtain, and I peeked out. He had really done his job. Every seat in the house was taken, clear up to the top balcony, and he informed me that there were lines of people out front who could not get in.

I was nervous but raring to go. Soon we were underway, and soon I was in trouble. My problem was similar to the one Lot's wife had; I kept looking back. I'd barely get past one problem when, thinking back over it, I'd get caught unprepared with another problem inundating me like an ocean wave.

The more problems I had, the more I'd perspire. Then my glasses would slip down my nose, and I'd have to take one hand out of circulation to push them back into place. Meanwhile, out on the tip of my nose, they were in a perfect position to catch three or four splats of perspiration rolling off my brow. Every aria and chorus seemed like one I'd never seen before. My eyes were just not recognizing the notes, and my mind could not recall any tempos. The recitatives were especially unfamiliar. Sometimes I'd just throw a downbeat and wait to see what would come out.

Finally it was over, and the applause was deafening. I turned around to take a bow as I had been instructed to do and realized that not only were my garters down; they had brought the socks down with them. There they flapped like a pair of dangling spats. But who cared? I had lived through my first performance of Handel's *Messiah,* and we had all ended together!

nine

THE BIG TIME

The last half of the 1950s impress me as the time that recordings of gospel music really took a giant step forward. At that time my work, as I have said, was mainly with Earle Williams of Sacred Records and Hugh Edwards, owner of Alma Records (the new label name for International Records). If there were any other labels in existence, I didn't know it.

Also, there was considerable tension between the traditional and the contemporary camps. They didn't know what to call each other, so often they resorted to dumb labels such as "worldly," "modern" and "sacrilegious" on the traditional side and "old fogey," "dark ages," and "stodgy" on the contemporary side.

Personally, I thought there was a time and place for all kinds of music. But at the same time, I got a kick out of the controversy and found myself experimenting with new things. And usually what I tried was considered "worldly." There were gospel bookstores that banned our recordings, and many radio stations, including the Moody station in Chicago, absolutely refused to play records that featured Vangie or my group or band. Often, however, they had no choice but to play recordings on which I had done backgrounds; in those years, they didn't have a lot of choice.

What fond memories and fast friendships I brought out of that era! Someday when we all get over in Glory, I'm gonna line them up and do a mammoth '50s concert. The program will read like this: Bill Carl, Allen McGill, Beth Farnham, Bob Daniels, Les Barnett, Georgia Lee, Rudy Atwood, Gloria Roe, Homer Rodeheaver, the Good Twins, Jack

Holcomb, Stuart Hamblen, John Gustafson, The Sunday Sing Trio, George Beverly Shea, *The Baptist Laymen's Hour* choir, Loren Whitney, Charles Magnuson, Charlie Turner, The Sons of Song, Frank Alpers, and Ben and Beth Allen. For a finale, I'll have the Ty Brothers Quartet sing with the band the arrangement of "When The Saints Go Marching In" that was released in 1950 on one of the old Campus Christian Hour recordings and was promptly banned everywhere!

Yes, those were great days, but they couldn't last forever, and they didn't. Toward the end of the decade, things started happening that propelled me in a different direction for a while.

On a tour with *The Baptist Laymen's Hour,* I was taken aside by our host in Washington, D.C. He said that he had gotten one of the records I had recorded for Bob Daniels and he was disappointed in the sound because the orchestra sounded thin. He felt Bob had a great voice and deserved better.

He said, "Now, you take this recording on RCA Victor by Hugo Winterhalter—there's a real sound. Why don't you listen to his writing and see if you can get some tips?"

Well, I knew how Hugo wrote—and David Rose, and Andre Kostalonetz and Gordon Jenkins. And, arrogant as always, I figured I knew full well what the difference was. I had been stuck with three violins and three rhythm on the Bob Daniels album in question while the major studios always used a minimum of twenty strings (twelve violins, four violas, four cellos).

I couldn't wait to get home. I never wanted to record with three violins again—not ever! I plied Earle Williams with every persuasive trick I knew, and I finally talked him into recording with some real, honest-to-goodness orchestras. One such recording was called *Rhapsody in Sacred Music.*

And then I got to record a big-choir album as well. It featured twenty-five of the best voices in Hollywood. (That's a "big choir" as far as recording is concerned!) I had Loulie Jean Norman on lead soprano and Thurl Ravenscroft on low bass and all the other good guys in between. I wrote for them just as I'd write for an orchestra, and they sightread it. It was almost frightening! The album was first released on Sacred under the title, *The Garden of The Heart.* It has since been rereleased on the Light label under the title, *The Savior Is Waiting.*

Now I had the sounds I wanted. I hoped never to be unfavorably compared again. I had to have the numbers of voices and instruments with which to work, and I intended to have them at all costs. But that was the problem—costs. I didn't know anything about the economics of the gospel recording business, and I'm afraid I didn't care to know. Naturally, it cost a lot less to make a record back then, but the potential sales were a lot smaller also. The average record probably sold around two thousand copies; a good record sold about five thousand; and a smash hit would have been ten thousand sales. (Today an artist may sell a hundred thousand or more.) Most artists sold more recordings in their meetings or concerts than were sold through "store distribution."

My demands at Sacred Records were unreasonable; I can see that now. Not only did I want an unheard-of budget, but the music I wanted to record was just not in demand. The few people who liked it *really* liked it. But the many people who didn't like it disliked it a whole lot, and said so. After we recorded the *Rhapsody* album, the costs were so high and the criticism so severe that everything just came to a halt for a while. I believe Earle would have mortgaged his home to keep funding my experiments, but his board of directors at Sacred Records just put their collective foot down and said, "We don't need that kind of music. And on top of that, we can't afford it!"

It was many months before I again recorded an instrumental album for Earle, but it was worth the wait for me. There was a recording called *101 Strings* that was getting a lot of airplay, and I sold Earle on the idea of doing an album called *102 Strings*. But I'm getting ahead of my story. . . .

That July I was invited to be musical director at Youth For Christ International, which was held in the great Billy Sunday Tabernacle in Winona Lake, Indiana. Dr. Harnish gave me the time off. It was a terrific experience for me as day after day we rehearsed and night after night I conducted the five-hundred-voice choir, accompanied by sixteen trumpets, twelve trombones, and a half-dozen baritones and tubas. We would sandwich the visiting celebrity singers and musicians into what we called "a musical package," and then end with everyone on stage for a finale. Then, during the late, late night, I'd write the arrangements for the next day.

One night I had some guys take a couple of tubs full of dry ice up on the roof next to the open-air vents. When we got to the last chorus of this particular song about heaven, they were to dump buckets of water over the dry ice. They were right on cue, and with a sizzle and a roar, here came the white clouds pouring into the auditorium. The problem was, it looked more like smoke than clouds, and it wasn't long before we heard the sirens of the Warsaw, Indiana, volunteer fire truck as it rumbled to a stop alongside the building.

I think the kids loved the music. But the phrase, "It sounds too much like Hollywood," began to drift through to my ears, and when the week was over I came back to the coast with my hackles up.

When I returned from Indiana, there was a message waiting for me from Max Herman, whom I had met while doing *Mr. Texas* and *Oiltown, U.S.A.* He was in the music business and was Redd Harper's publisher. When I returned his call, he asked me if I would like to write some big-band arrangements for *The Frankie Lane Show*. I had never written anything like that, but I had wanted to, and here was the chance I'd waited for. I tried to keep my voice steady and talk slowly as I told Max I thought I could fit the job into my busy schedule.

Max said that Harry Zimmerman (Frankie Lane's conductor) was waiting for me to call and that he would give me further instructions. When I arrived at Harry's, there was another arranger there also waiting to pick up an assignment; he introduced himself as Hank Mancini. When my turn came to talk to Harry, I decided to be as close to mute as possible, because the only way Harry would know I had never done anything like this before would be if I said something stupid. He gave me eleven titles, Frankie's range, the instrumentation, his copyist's number, and a deadline.

The prerecording session was in two weeks. I buried myself in pencils and manuscript and went at it tooth and nail. Vangie said I probably ought to get a haircut before the date, since I was writing for a big star and all. So the day before the session I drove into Sy Devore's on Vine Street and was sitting in Art's barber chair when in walked Harry Zimmerman.

Art had the barber sheet wrapped around my neck, and my long hair was going every which way. Harry kept eyeing me, then suddenly he said, "Hey, aren't you the kid writing some Frankie Lane things?"

I said, "Yes, sir."

He said, "Are you done?"

I said, "I'm on the last one."

He said, "Get out of here, Don't you know the date's tomorrow?"

Back at The Little Church of Sherman Oaks, I wound up in time to get a few hours of fitful sleep, which was a few hours more than the copyist got. The next morning I showed up at an old theatre over on Wilshire Boulevard where the recording and filming was to take place. I could hear the band tuning up as I pushed through the swinging doors from the darkened lobby into the empty theatre and slid into a rear seat. My heart was in my throat, hoping that the arrangements would sound OK.

As it turned out, I wouldn't have needed that haircut. I never met Frankie. Harry didn't even see me. In fact, no one saw me, but it didn't matter—not one bit. They loved the charts. After, and sometimes during, each run-through, Frankie would glide over to Harry and back-slap him, and they would laugh and do a little body English in time to one of the brass licks. For all Frankie knew, Harry had written those charts, and Harry didn't bother to tell him otherwise.

Two weeks of writing and it was all over in a few hours. Then I thought how nice it was not to have anybody say, "Hey, that sounds worldly." But at the same time I felt a little uneasy; I was in strange territory. And at one point a fleeting doubt popped across my mind as to whether or not I'd be in trouble if Christ should return at that very moment.

I learned more about writing for a band in those two weeks than I had learned during my whole life up until that time, and I picked up a check for almost twelve hundred dollars after taxes. Just think—I was being paid union scale and being educated at the same time. I remembered every fill, every line, every chord change and every modulation, and I thought that some day I was going to use all of those same devices in gospel music. They would work; I just knew it. But getting them accepted would take time and patience.

(Incidentally, years later, while I was doing the Roy Rogers/Dale Evans Saturday-night TV specials, Harry Zimmerman did some ghost-writing for me. And I finally told him that he had given me my first secular arranging job on the Frankie Lane Show. He laughed and said, "It's too late to do anything about it now!")

Soon I got another call from Max Herman. This time I was to get in touch with Elliot Daniels, the composer and arranger for the *I Love Lucy* and *December Bride* TV shows. He had been elected president of the union and would need some help on his two shows.

The following Saturday I met with Elliot, who was very businesslike. He said, "Here's the way we will work. I'll get the timings from the editor and sketch the cues; then you will orchestrate them and get them to the copyist." I agreed. But about the second week into the series, Elliot called and said he was getting too busy to do the composing; would I like to take a crack at it? I said I'd be happy to. After a few more weeks, I started getting the timings from the editor by phone. I thought, "Wouldn't it be nice if I could phone my part in?" but I never was able to manage it. That was the final season for both of those shows, but working on them taught me an awful lot about scoring that has helped me through the years. And I got paid union scale to boot.

I'm pretty sure that by this time my music was close to being an obsession with me. Perhaps it had been for a long time. Our family didn't do the things most families do. We went to church to make music. We went to neighboring towns to make music. We had people over to talk about the music on the next recording. We met new people only if they were in the music business. We went to social gatherings if music people would be there. Neither Vangie nor I had hobbies—not alone or together. Our hobby was music. We didn't picnic or hike. We didn't play tennis or golf. My love for horses had long since become just a childhood fantasy. When I prayed, it was usually about music: "Dear God, help me do a good job on this recording, and don't forget to bless that other project. . . ."

Our marriage had become a triangle, with music as the third party. We were more like competitive brother and sister than husband and wife. Poor little Carol was being terribly cheated out of all the good things families are supposed to do and have.

The crazy thing about it was that I didn't realize this was happening. As long as the phone kept ringing, I was happy, and I interpreted that as God's blessing. I figured that God's main interest in me was what I could do for Him, and boy, was I doing it! I took every offer that came along. My game plan was to learn from the secular field and write all the pop music I could. At the same time, I'd take every opportunity that was offered in the Christian field to introduce what I was learning from the secular.

One day I received a call from a guy named Buddy Cole, who was a phenomenal keyboard player. I had been using him in some of my recording sessions. Buddy was also musical director for Rosemary Clooney. Miss Clooney was enjoying one hit after another at that time, so you can imagine my surprise when Buddy said, "She wants to record a hymn album, and I don't know how to write that church stuff. Would you write and conduct the album?"

I did it. We used choir and rhythm, and it came out on the Columbia label. Almost immediately Buddy called again. This time he asked me to be the choral director and arranger on a Bing Crosby TV special. Buddy had a great band, and I had a great twenty-one-voice chorus. One of our guests was Mahalia Jackson, and she was some kind of singer. There was a ballad that I had arranged featuring the choir and a duo of ballet dancers. Mr. Crosby liked it very much and said so. This pleased me no end since I had found out I had gotten the job because Norman Luboff was not available.

Word was getting out about my secular work, and I felt the sting of rebuff from many of my old friends and associates. After the Bing Crosby show, on which I got screen credit, my ordination was not renewed. They didn't refuse my application, but it was just suggested that I not apply for renewal.

In 1958 the new Capitol Towers were completed in Hollywood, and that is where we recorded the *Rhapsody in Sacred Music* album I had finally persuaded Earle Williams to make. Val Valentino, who mixed the album, asked if he could have a copy and, flattered, I gave him two. A few weeks later he was on a plane to Cuba to do the mixing on the Nat King Cole recording, *Cole Español*. On the plane he sat next to Nat's producer, Lee Gillette, and ended up telling him of our *Rhapsody* sessions and giving him an album.

When they returned, Lee Gillette called and asked me to meet him. I had seen him roaming the halls of Capitol, and he seemed to do a lot of hollering and cussing, so I was more than a little uncertain about our first meeting. But he wasn't half bad. He said he had listened to my record and if that's what they played in my church, he wouldn't mind going. He also asked how an ordained minister learned how to write like that. I told him I had learned "the hard way." That seemed to satisfy him.

It wasn't long after our meeting that I was in the studio with a forty-five-piece orchestra and a twenty-five-voice choir recording a Christmas album with Nat King Cole. I found out later that I got the job because they couldn't get their first choice, Gordon Jenkins. That didn't matter one bit to me. It was a great break, and I gave it all I had. Here I was with seventy of the world's top singers and instrumentalists in a state-of-the-art studio, with one of the best producers in Hollywood and the greatest pop singer of our time, recording the Christmas carols telling of the Savior's birth. And Capitol Records was picking up the tab. Once again, I was learning and getting paid at the same time!

Things really started happening then. The calls came in right and left, and I still wouldn't turn anything down. Over the next few years I wrote and/or conducted for Peggy Lee, Jack Jones, Stan Kenton, Count Basie, Duke Ellington, Earl (Fatha) Hines, Kay Starr, Roger Williams, Stuart Hamblen, Sue Raney, Barbara McNair, Debbie Reynolds, Alvino Rey, The King Sisters, Pat Boone, Eddie Fisher, Julie London, Jimmy Durante, Margaret Whiting, Shani Wallis, Shirley Bassey, Pete Fountain, Jane Powell, Al Martino, Tex Ritter, George Shearing, Clint Walker, Lena Horne, Allen Sherman, Pete Barbuti, Frank Gorshin, Stan Freberg, Don Rickles, Red Skelton, Ben Blue, Frankie Lane, Bing Crosby ("Do You Hear What I Hear?"), and Ella Fitzgerald. I worked for Capitol, Decca, Kapp, RCA, and Columbia. I wrote all kinds of music under all kinds of conditions (mostly pressure). I also ghosted for David Rose, Billy May, Les Baxter, Jud Conlin, Walter Shumann, Bobby Hammack, and Ray Heindorf. In addition to *I Love Lucy* (Lucille Ball) and *December Bride,* (Spring Byington), I was music director on some other TV shows such as *My Mother the Car* (Jerry Van Dyke) and *OK Crackerby* (Burl Ives). I also worked on some films, including *Finnian's Rainbow* (Fred Astaire, Petula Clark), *The 4-D Man* (Robert Lansing), and *The Blob* (Steve McQueen).

There was no doubt that I was learning on the job, and all the things I learned in the secular field I'd try to find a way to use in the gospel field. Sometimes it would work, and sometimes it wouldn't. Occasionally a gospel artist with whom I had worked with for years would say, "Now that you're writing 'worldly' music for Nat Cole, I don't want to use you anymore on my recording sessions." And that was that.

I'm a firm believer in "repeat business," and it always hurt to lose somebody. I watched other arrangers who would only work for an artist one time. By and by, they would run out of artists and be out of work. I liked to get an artist, producer, or company and keep him or her. Then, when I added another, I'd have twice the business.

I would seldom tell one artist or producer about another artist or producer. People like to think they are the only ones you are working for. I once had a copyist who, everytime I called him, would recite his calendar for the month to me before he'd take the job. That annoyed me, and I figured it would surely annoy an artist or a producer. One time I had *four* Christian film projects for four different producers during a four-month period—Dick Ross, Bill Brusseau, Ken Anderson and Shorty Yeaworth. I don't think any one of them knew I was working for the other until it was over.

In the late 1950s, Vangie and I moved from our little apartment and bought a comfortable three-bedroom home in Van Nuys. It was north of Ventura Boulevard, which denotes its modesty, but it was a step up for the Carmichaels.

When we bought our little house, the folks gave us the old family upright piano on which Sis and I had taken lessons when we were kids. With a piano in the house, I didn't have to be away all night writing. The best part was that it meant the family was together more. Even though Vangie and Carol didn't get a lot of attention, at least they were aware of a living presence under their roof. They got so used to the sound of the piano through the night that they would wake up if I quit playing for any length of time.

One of the best things about our new house was that it was located very close to Dick Ross, for whom I was working regularly on various film projects. The Billy Graham Evangelistic Association had taken over Great Commission Films, changing the name to World Wide Pictures, and Dick was now producing films almost exclusively for Dr. Graham.

It was during this period of time that I resigned as minister of music at Temple Baptist Church. It didn't happen suddenly, but it happened.

I can remember when the problem started. I was writing on two assignments at once (which had become par for the course in those days) and had worked through the night on Saturday, right up until it was time to head downtown to Temple for the morning worship service.

A quick shave and shower got the adrenalin going, and with some family conversation I managed the freeway drive without falling asleep. During Sunday school I hunkered down like a turtle and was glad for a little peaceful solitude as I shut out the other sounds in the room. Soon I was in my choir robe and moving like a robot through the morning service. Then Dr. Harnish was preaching, and within thirty seconds I was asleep. Whether I snored or missed my cue for the invitation song I can't remember, but I had committed the unpardonable.

If it had only happened once, even the unpardonable may have been pardoned. But as the weeks went by, it became more and more obvious that my priorities were undergoing a change.

This was not the same situation I had experienced at Inglewood; the problem was not my attitude, nor was it disdain for the volunteer musicians. I loved them and appreciated their sacrifices in terms of time and effort. I viewed their capabilities in perspective and kept my professional expectations totally separate from the ministry of the church staff.

The problem was simply that I was being offered opportunities that I could not refuse and there were not enough hours in the day. So I was giving fewer and fewer of those hours to my job. I would ask to be excused from choir rehearsal, leaving the choir president in charge. Then I would miss the publishing deadline for the "order of service" in the church bulletin. And I began nodding off during service on a more frequent basis. Finally I resigned. Although Dr. Harnish was no longer my boss, he remained my friend, and one of the best.

I continued to direct *The Baptist Laymen's Hour,* because their recording schedule had been reduced to twice monthly, at which time we would record two programs at one sitting. But with that exception, my whole efforts were now directed at writing and arranging.

How wonderful to be able to write around the clock, uninterrupted, day after day! I went at it like a hog at the trough. But in the process I developed even more of a one-track mind than before. Mine was an obviously selfish existence. I hardly missed the circle of friends from Temple Baptist. I seldom remembered birthdays or anniversaries. Carol would say, "Daddy, can we play?" I'd say, "Not now honey; go away, Daddy's busy." Vangie and I talked less and less. I'd see her at recording sessions if there was a choral group used.

In January 1960, a series of events occurred that made me really stop and think about my life. I was doing an album for Capitol Records with Alvino Rey. All the songs were slow, sad ballads; Lee Gillette said they were going to title the album, *That Lonely Feeling.* Southern California was in the middle of a flu epidemic, and I sure didn't want to catch it because the "show must go on" was part of my work ethic. The band was all set for Monday morning, January 18, and I still had a lot of notes to write.

At the time, my dear, godly mother-in-law, Frieda Otto, was terminally ill with cancer and was at Hollywood Presbyterian Hospital. Vangie was staying at her bedside. My dad had the flu, but just a week earlier he had helped Mom fix egg pancakes for us at their apartment, and he said he'd be better in a few days.

At about nine o'clock on Sunday night, the phone rang. Vangie said Frieda was failing rapidly and I should get there as soon as possible. Just as I was going out the door, the phone rang again. But this time it was Mom, calling to say that the paramedics were taking Dad to a hospital in Southgate. I called Vangie back, told her what had happened, and headed the car toward Southgate. When I arrived, they had Dad under oxygen, but his condition was stable. His lungs had filled with fluid and his heart had stopped, but the paramedics had whopped him a good one on the chest and he had started breathing again.

While waiting around feeling helpless, I called Vangie to check on Frieda. She was about the same, and since I still had work to do, it was decided that I should go on home. Dad was resting "easy," so finally I headed back to the Valley. I walked into the darkened house, crossed over to the piano, and numbly started to write.

A few minutes before three in the morning, the stillness was shattered by the phone. Dad had suddenly taken a turn for the worse: "come immediately." I set the receiver back in the cradle, and it rang again. It was Vangie. Through her tears she said that Frieda had just passed away. When I told her about Dad, she said that she would meet me in Southgate. By the time we got there, Dad, too, had gone to be with the Lord he had served so faithfully all his life.

I have forgotten the details of the next hour or so, but as the sun started to brush back the darkness of night, I was back at the piano, trying to see the notes through my tears. The song I was arranging was "It's a Lonesome Old Town When You're Not Around." Later that morning in the studio at Capitol, I cried again when we played it.

That afternoon I picked Carol up from school and took her to Bob's Big Boy for a hamburger. She had slept through the night without knowing what had transpired, and now I had to tell her. It was not easy.

Losing Dad was the single greatest loss of my life. I did a lot of thinking after that. I thought about the foolishness of our lives—so much of it was not really living at all. Much of what people struggle, connive, and fight for is just not worth the effort we put into it.

I began to sort out in my mind the things that were precious enough to die for. I saw myself in front of a firing squad while an inquisitor confronted me with all the things I had thought were dear to me. I mean everything, both abstract and tangible—faith, theological doctrines, ethics, integrity, morals, lifestyle, pleasure, work, friends, family, worldly possessions, reputation. As the imaginary inquisitor paraded each one by, I was asked to give it up or die.

He'd say, "How about this one? Are you willing to die for this?" The guns would come to firing position, and I'd weigh it in my mind and say, "Well, I believe I can get along without that." The guns would lower. Then he'd say, "And how about this item?" I'd say, "No, you can't take that away." And then I'd hear the hammers click back, and I would know that item was really important to me—important enough to die for.

When it was all over, I had a pretty short list. I'm not going to tell you everything that was on it, and I'm not sure my list is quite the same today. But I will tell you that high up on the list was keeping the original deal I had made with God back in 1947—if He'd help with my music projects, He could have possession of them. *He* had sure kept his part of the bargain! But I wasn't too sure about my part. I had a lot more thinking to do about that.

ten

CLOSE CALLS

I was not writing just for the money, but I was making a lot of it. It somehow didn't seem equitable that I could make as much money arranging and conducting one session as my father had made in a whole year preaching. Vangie was also doing very well financially, singing at recording sessions and on TV shows. Soon we were house shopping again.

This time we bought a large, new home south of Ventura Boulevard in Encino. (Those of you who know the San Fernando Valley will recognize "south of the boulevard" and "Encino" as highly prized status symbols of the '60s.) The place came complete with fireplace, a pool, a view, and a maid's quarters that would serve as my office. And the work went on.

I signed a recording contract with Capitol Records to do my own pop records. Lee Gillette was my boss at Capitol. He produced many artists and would call me often to write and conduct the sessions he produced.

By this time I was doing all of Nat King Cole's recordings and road shows. Gillette had given me a release to work for Roger Williams, who was on another label called Kapp Records. So Nat and Roger became my main accounts. They were both top sellers, so the budgets were unlimited, the bands were large, and the music was fun. In between sessions with Nat and Roger, I would work for other artists and do films and television. I thought I had it all. The adrenalin flowed high, and I worked day and night.

To help keep me going, I begin to take pills. I discovered some high protein pills that seemed to work wonders. I'll not mention the name brand because I think they finally took it off the market. At any rate, I would take a double ration of these on a daily basis. If I still needed more zip, I'd take Dexamyl, which I believe was a cross between Dexedrine and Miltown. It was supposed to perk you up and keep you calm all at the same time.

With so many assignments, I lived in constant fear of missing a deadline. I had developed a reputation for working well under pressure, being a fast writer, and never missing a deadline. Naturally, I liked that reputation and even helped perpetuate it. The problem was that I started to believe it myself. And that put me in line for some close calls.

I particularly remember a time when I had been up all night finishing a film score that was to record at nine o'clock the next morning. The copyists had worked alongside me through the night. At eight o'clock, I only had one cue left to write, but it was a long one—over four minutes in length.

It was a scene in a hospital operating room, with the doctor and his assistant working over a patient whose life hung in the balance. I could easily have spent a whole day composing and arranging four minutes' worth of film music for a large orchestra, but I didn't have a whole day; I had one hour. I also had a five-day growth of beard and was desperately in need of a shower. Besides, I'd have to be lucky to make the studio by nine o'clock through the morning freeway traffic. I told the copyists to pack up and meet me at the studio.

Have you ever shaved and showered in six minutes? I did it. I grabbed a handful of sharpened pencils and a pad of eight-bar score paper, backed out of the driveway, and headed for the freeway, telling myself how great I felt. I almost believed it.

Settling into traffic, I picked up the cue sheets and read through them with one eye—the other eye was on the taillight of the car in front of me. There must have been a hundred things to catch in the descriptive timings the film editor had prepared for me.

I realized there was no way I could treat this like an ordinary cue and write it in traffic in the next three-quarters of an hour. So I thought I would try something ridiculous. The scene seemed to have one very noticeable characteristic that remained constant throughout—mounting tension. Then, at the very end, everyone would glance at the electronic screen monitoring the heartbeat, the head surgeon would give the OK sign, and the tension would be over.

So, first, some arithmetic. Four minutes and four seconds is two hundred forty-four seconds. The easiest way to chew that up is to use a twenty-four-frame click track, which is four seconds to the bar.* So, dividing four into two hundred forty-four means that sixty-one bars will be needed to complete the cue.

At the bottom of the eight-bar score paper I marked the cumulative seconds for each bar: four, eight, twelve, sixteen, and so on—all the way through the sixty-one bars. That took seven full pages and an eighth page with five bars left over. Then, checking the cue sheets, I found significant places along the way to increase the tension and marked those at the bottom of the pages, using my cumulative timings as guide-posts. So far, I hadn't written a note, but what I had done was just as important as the notes.

Next I did a one-bar tympani pattern and indicated to the copyist that it should continue throughout, ending on the downbeat of bar sixty-one. Next, I started putting notes on the page without regard to pitch, rhythm, tonality, harmonies, time values—or anything. In front of some I'd put sharps; in front of others I'd put flats.

At first they were whole notes sparsely placed and just on the violin, viola, cello, and Arco bass** staffs. At a given point partway into the cue, I added notes on the woodwind staffs for contrabass clarinet, bass clarinet, English horn, oboe, and Bb clarinet. Then, a little further on, I added notes for trombones and French horns and finally for trumpets.

I thought of the score paper as a canvas and the marks I was making as a picture of a storm painted with circles and dots, some on the lines and some on the spaces. Sometimes I'd miss and you couldn't tell if a note was on a line or a space. As I got further into the cue, the density of the notes increased, until by the last couple of bars everyone was playing a sustained tone—a nameless chord with clusters of minor seconds. It would be an ugly cacophony of sound with the pulse of the tympani pounding through it all until bar sixty-one, when everything would stop except one lone clarinet tone that carried on through to fade out at the end of the cue.

You can get killed doing what I had done. I don't recommend it. I pulled into the parking lot, double parked, and dashed for the studio, leaving the keys in the car. The copyists gathered around me while the orchestra tuned up. I explained to them that they were about to

---

* A click track is an electronic timing device which makes a clicking sound in the headset worn by each musician and which regulates the tempo of the cue being recorded.

** A bass played with a bow.

have the thrill of a lifetime. They were going to copy this picture of a gathering storm I had drawn with circles and dots. I told them that if there was a doubt as to whether a circle or dot was on a space or a line, they should put it on both. None of my notes had stems, so I said to add them at will. Also, once an instrument made an entrance, it was to play something, anything, until the downbeat of bar sixty-one, and "Good luck; you've got two hours and forty-five minutes to finish."

The date went well. Dick Ross didn't complain about anything, which meant he was tickled to death with the score. Finally we were down to the end of the session, and over the intercom Dick said, "Hey, we're missing the 'operating room' cue."

At that very moment, the copyists walked through the door and passed the music out. I set the digital clock for twenty-four frames, and everyone put their click-track headsets on. I counted off a slow four and we were off. We recorded the first run-through, and it was a take. The guys in the band applauded and yelled, "Yo, Ralph." Dick walked out of the control room and said, "Great, just great." I couldn't believe what had just happened.

Of course, that wasn't the only time I made a deadline by a hair. On the ground floor of the Capitol Towers building there are three recording studios: A, B, and C. Running through the catacomb of studios and control booths is a long L-shaped hallway, at the end of which is a very special room designated only by the word *Men* on the door. Inside, against the back wall, are two private cubicles. More times than I care to admit, I have fled to the quiet solitude of one of these cubicles with pencil and score paper in hand to complete the last arrangement for a session then in progress.

Of all the hundreds of deadlines I have lived through, I can recall only two that ended in disaster. The first was a morning session for Roger Williams. It involved a large orchestra, and we were going to record three sides from ten in the morning to one in the afternoon— a three-hour date. The copyist, Irv Wright, came to my house at seven o'clock in the morning, at which time he handed me the first completed arrangement neatly stacked inside the score. I in turn handed him the score to the second arrangement and told him I would bring the third arrangement to the session and he could pick it up there. At about one minute to ten, I stepped into the studio and handed Irv arrangement number three, and he took off with it.

The first tune went great. Roger was animated; and Dave Kapp, the producer, was unusually friendly. I have never seen Dave when he didn't have on a tailored suit, a starched collar, a silk tie, a fresh haircut, and a manicure. This morning was no exception. He was a very articulate man and ran his sessions like a corporate officer.

We took a ten-minute break after the first tune, and I was sweating blue bullets waiting for the next tune to arrive. It did—just in time to be passed out before the break was over. So far, so good. However, that was the last good thing that happened that day. The third tune never did show up. The last half-hour of the date, the band stood around with nothing to play. I did the usual things—kept calling Irv and drinking coffee. I said the usual things—"It will be here any minute; there must have been an accident on the freeway."

About an hour into overtime, Dave Kapp called me into the control booth. Roger was standing there and could tell something was coming. Dave's face was beet-red as he lifted his voice to proclaim, "You are an incompetent, bungling jerk, and you will never work in this town again."

Irv never did finish copying. The band was dismissed, and we all went home.

It was a terrible experience. But I not only kept working in town; I worked for both Roger Williams and Dave Kapp again. In fact, shortly after that disastrous day, Dave called me to work for Jack Jones and then Shani Wallis, and he signed me as an artist on the Kapp Records label. However, I never missed another deadline for Mr. Kapp.

The other deadline catastrophe occurred in Philadelphia on the Nat Cole recording of the *My Fair Lady* album. We were using a forty-five-piece orchestra and a sixteen-voice choir. The dates were scheduled for Tuesday, Wednesday, and Thursday afternoons, and we were to record at the Philadelphia Athletic Club. That seemed like a strange place to record, but the Philadelphia Symphony recorded there, and everyone said the sound was great.

I arrived in town Sunday night with about half the album written, and I went right to work finishing up. Irv Wright, my copyist from the West Coast, flew in a day later and set up shop in his hotel room, copying as I wrote. The first two sessions went fine, with a lot of back-slapping and compliments all around. Irv had rounded up some help; he had found two guys from Philadelphia. They were pretty slow, but Irv said not to worry; he'd get the last tune to me before we took our last ten-minute break.

There was a big press party with food and everything planned for immediately after the session upstairs in the plush Club Room. In addition to the press, a lot of disc jockeys and other friends and fans of

Nat King Cole from the Philly area were invited. The date was going well and Nat was feeling chipper. He was dressed up all dapper, wearing his little checkered hat with the narrow brim and kidding around, pretending he was Rex Harrison.

Lee Gillette said, "Let's take our break, and then when we come back we'll do the last tune" (which was "On The Street Where You Live.") Hy Lesnick, the contractor who had hired all of the musicians, came over and said, "Where's the music?" I said, "Keep an eye on that door. It will be walking in any minute. In the meantime, call Irv at the hotel just to make sure." Everybody was in a very happy mood, but I was holding off for a few minutes until that last arrangement arrived.

Well, you guessed it. The music never did arrive—not that afternoon, anyway. Hy came back from the phone with the news that it would be at least another fifteen minutes. Then it was another fifteen minutes, and then another. Finally, with the hot hors d'oeuvres getting cold and all the dignitaries milling around, I saw Lee go over to Nat. They were looking at their watches, and I glanced at mine. It was coming up on half-past five. We were already a half-hour into overtime, which is double scale, with no music in sight. Lee and Nat were moving in my direction, and I figured, "Oh boy, here it comes."

Now, Mr. Cole either wouldn't or couldn't pronounce the *L* in *Ralph*. So he said, "Raff, these Philadelphia copyists really loused us up good, didn't they?" I glanced at Lee, and he seemed unusually interested in the shine on his shoes. Nat continued, "Let's break the band now and call everybody back tomorrow." Then, with a grin he said, "That last tune better be good. . . . Come on, let's go up to the party."

Later that evening, Lee and I had dinner at Bookbinder's. Not a word was said about the disaster during dinner. We had just gotten out of the cab and were walking toward the front entrance of the hotel. The wind was blowing and there were few passersby that time of night.

Suddenly Lee stepped in front of me and, grabbing the lapels of my overcoat, stuck his walrus mustache in my face and growled, "The band thinks it was the copyists' fault, and Nat thinks it was the copyists' fault, but you and I know it's your fault that Nat has to pay for bringing that whole band back for one lousy tune."

I've had many other close calls since, but I never again missed a deadline on any of Gillette's dates from that time on.

Many of the secular artists I worked for showed a genuine interest in my profession as a Christian, and for others my ministerial background was just a curiosity. Peggy Lee nicknamed me "Rev"; Robert

Mitchum called me "Deacon." Sitting in a booth at the old Formosa Cafe after recording the Kenton Christmas album, Stan declared, "Carmichael, if I can help sell Jesus with my band, I'm all for it. God knows the world could use a little more Christianity."

One of the most beautiful and sensitive albums I ever recorded with Roger Williams was made up entirely of old hymns, which he picked out himself. Incidentally, Roger was a preacher's kid.

One day during a planning session for a Nat King Cole road show, Mr. Cole (also a preacher's kid) said out of the blue, "Hey, how about doing a whole segment of spirituals." We did, and it turned out to be one of the highlights of the show. It included "Let It Be, Dear Lord," "Nobody Knows the Trouble I've Seen," "When The Saints Go Marching In," "Get On Board, Little Children" and several others. Nat was going to take a twelve-voice choir on the road, so I wrote the arrangements for the medley, making special use of the voices. It was staged with the choir in robes and Nat dressed in a black "Sunday go to meetin' " suit and tie. Flashed on the backdrop curtain was a lighting effect showing a silhouette of the cross.

When the show played in the main room at the Sands Hotel in Las Vegas, Jack Entrater, who ran the Sands, told Nat he wanted the "church bit" cut. Nat said, "Either the spiritual medley stays in or you'll have to find yourself another boy singer." The afternoon after opening night, several of us, including Mr. Entrater and Mr. Cole, were in the Athletic Club. We had taken steam baths and were having our rubdowns when suddenly Mr. Entrater raised up and hollered over in Nat's direction, "You know, that 'church thing' is great. I'm glad we decided to leave it in."

To say that opening nights were not exciting would be an outright lie. But they were also traumatic, and I was always relieved when they were behind me. After opening night at the Greek Theatre in Los Angeles, Nat called me into his dressing room. We had gotten through the evening in pretty good shape, and I was feeling rather satisfied with the whole affair. But when I stepped through the door, Nat said, "Push it shut" in a tone of voice that didn't sound too friendly.

"How come you didn't take a bow after the overture?" he said. "Don't you know this is a class joint?" I promised to take a bow the next night, which I did. But after the show Mr. Cole called me in again. "Raff, do you call that a bow?" he said. "I was watching through the curtain, and it looked more like a curtsy, and if I had blinked, I would have missed it. And besides, you have to wait until the spotlight hits you. Now, look, here's the way you do it."

We rehearsed bows a few times till I had it right. The next night, after the overture, I turned around, paused a beat, and bent at the middle until I could touch my toes. The applause was twice what it was the two previous nights, and I knew I had turned in an excellent bow. There was no more said about bows, and to this day I guess I still have a simple formula for a good overture. End on a high note and take a deep bow, and you've got it made.

Opening night at the San Juan Intercontinental Hotel in Puerto Rico was a dilly. Only two guys in the band spoke English.

Opening night at the Geary Theatre in San Francisco was a panic. It was a show called, *I'm With You,* and there were twenty-four in the cast, including Nat. The producer, director, and choreographer were making changes right up until curtain time. The copyists kept bringing in music until seven forty-five.

The door should have been opened at seven, but they kept the crowd waiting outside until just a few minutes before showtime. Half the band played the show in street clothes, and I put my tux on without shaving and showering. We got through it, but I don't know how.

Opening night at the Waldorf Astoria in New York City with Roger Williams was well prepared and elegant. Opening night at the Fontainebleau in Miami with Debbie Reynolds was the same as the above except for one little problem. After rehearsal I had a bite to eat and went to my room to dress. There was plenty of time. I came down at about eight minutes to showtime, figuring to enter through the main entrance.

In the lobby were two long queues of people in tuxes and gowns, waiting to be seated. I walked to the head of the left line and started to say that I was in the show and needed to get backstage. But before I got the first word out, the bozo in the monkey suit said, "Go to the end of the line, mister." I moseyed back in that direction, glancing at my watch—still five minutes. Then I headed to the far side of the other line and moved up along the wall to the head of that queue, trying my luck with another "headwaiter" type. I said, "I'm leading the band tonight, and I need to get in." Bozo number one was looking over at us, and then he said, "Is that guy still trying to get in? Call the bouncer and have him thrown out."

Perspiration was pouring from my temples, and my collar was getting tighter by the minute. And speaking of minutes, I only had about two of them left. Finally I said, "Look, I'll give you twenty dollars if you'll have the bouncer take me backstage before he throws me out." The guy looked at the twenty I had produced, then back at my anguished

face, and said, "Maybe you are the band leader. Come on, follow me."
It was a great opening night.

During the early 1960s, I was music director on the Roy Rogers/
Dale Evans Saturday night specials that were aired weekly on the ABC
network. That's a grueling workload in itself, but every now and then
an album project or a film would come up, and then my life got really
hectic. I never turned anything down for fear they'd find somebody
else and I'd lose the account. So I depended on my protein pills and
my Dexamyls to keep on going.

Roger Williams called one day and said he wanted to record an
album. I said, "Great, I've been waiting for your call." We booked
the recording sessions around the TV rehearsal schedule, and finally
it was all done. I felt as if I'd been run over by a Mack truck.

The following Sunday afternoon, Vangie and I were invited down
to Palos Verdes to have dinner with some old friends from Temple
Baptist Church. I went through the paces feeling kind of numb, but
thankful that I had lived through the week. I figured I had been up
about sixty hours straight—thanks to my protein pills, a few Dexamyls,
and pots and pots of coffee.

Later that night in bed I reached over and shook Vangie. I said,
"There's something wrong."

She said, "What is it?"

"I think it's my heart."

Within about thirty seconds she was on the phone with our family
doctor, Ernie Stebbins. Within another couple of minutes we were
headed for his office. When we arrived, Dr. Stebbins was already there
getting the straps and gadgets ready to take an EKG. After the first
reading, he started flipping the straps off and said, "Let's go."

I said, "Where?"

He said, "To the hospital."

We went in his car. When we arrived, everyone was bustling around.
I got into bed and they put an oxygen mask on me, and the next
thirty minutes were taken up with one test after another. Pretty soon
I asked what was going on, and the doctor said I'd have to stay in
intensive care for the night, and that he'd be back first thing in the
morning. I asked him about doing my TV show, and he said I'd probably
done my last show for a few months. That night I was really scared.

Well, I did miss a couple of days of rehearsal, and I did have to
job out some of the writing, but I conducted the next show. When I
told the doctor what I had been doing lately, he said, "No wonder

107

you're having problems with your heart. You are suffering from extreme fatigue and your heart muscles were malfunctioning."

I never took any more protein pills or Dexamyls after that. I did carry a little container of glycerin tablets, and how comforting it was to know that Roy Rogers also had a little container of the same stuff. In fact, the following Saturday on the show we compared stories and pills.

eleven

CRUSADING

One day the phone rang, and a friendly voice said, "This is Ells Culver, and I'm calling for Dr. Bob Pierce. He would like to meet and talk." I thought to myself, "This must be more than a film or a concert." And it was!

At the meeting, Dr. Bob unfolded his dream of an Osaka Crusade, to be held at the Osaka Grand Opera House in the Osaka Grand Hotel— which is naturally in Osaka, Japan. He wanted to take with him a staff of musicians which would include several top gospel singers and their accompanists.

He wanted me to write new arrangements of a selected group of old hymns and gospel songs for a five-hundred-voice choir and a symphony orchestra. Then I'd go over a week early for combined rehearsals.

I said, "Dr. Bob, where are you going to get a symphony orchestra in Osaka, Japan?"

He turned to Ells Culver and said, "You can get one, can't you, Ells?"

Then I asked, "And what about the choir?"

Dr. Bob said, "Look, buddy, you leave the details to me. All I want to know is, do you want to go or not? It's going to be the one-hundredth anniversary of the Protestant church in Japan. World Vision is going to sponsor a celebration worthy of the occasion. And buddy, I just can't do it without you."

I thought, *Oh, Dr. Bob, you silver-tongued devil.* But I said, "I'd love to go, but you know, I've got this obligation and that obligation, and I'm writing a show that Nat King Cole wants to take to Broadway."

Oh boy, that did it! Dr. Bob hit the ceiling. Now, some people when they blow just go up in the direction of the ceiling, but Dr. Bob would really make contact. He gave me one of the best sermons I'd had in a long time. He reminded me that he had paid for my first big orchestra for a film score. He reminded me that he had paid for a big orchestra for my first network broadcast, an Easter sunrise service from the Pasadena Rose Bowl. He reminded me that I belonged to God in the first place. And he intimated that if I didn't go to Osaka, he dreaded to think of the consequences. Besides, he could afford to pay me more than I could make on any old Broadway show, so I had better pray about it!

The target date for the Osaka Crusade was about eight months down the road, but it only took me about eight hours to make up my mind. I knew Dr. Bob was absolutely right. All the things I had been learning were in preparation for an opportunity just like the one he was offering. I said I'd go, hoping that a one-month absence from the country could be worked out as smoothly as possible.

When the day approached, my schedule opened like the Red Sea, and I flew to Japan with a spirit of anticipation. Ells Culver secured the services of the Kyoto Symphony—seventy fine musicians. Under local leadership, many small choirs had been rehearsing the arrangements I had sent months in advance. And when they all came together, we had more than five hundred voices. The ten days of pre-crusade rehearsals were grueling but rewarding—even fun. The biggest problem was the language barrier, but we found ways to get around that.

The crusade ran nightly for two weeks, and each night we played and sang our hearts out to a packed opera house. The decor was breathtaking; the acoustics were as close to perfect as I have ever heard. Dr. Bob did some of the best preaching I'd ever heard, and the Japanese audiences responded as the invitation was given each night. But it wasn't only the Japanese who were responding; there was a response deep inside my own heart as well.

There were no deadlines during that crusade. All the writing had been done in advance; I had no need to burn the midnight oil. And still I spent sleepless nights. Maybe some of my insomnia was the result of prior conditioning. But some of it was caused by the fact that I had some thinking to do.

My little room at the Osaka Grand Hotel was about twenty steps away from the end of the corridor and a large double door that led into the suite occupied by Dr. Pierce and his lovely wife, Lorraine. About two o'clock one morning, I heard a light rapping on my door.

In response to my "Who's there?" Dr. Bob said, "Hey buddy, are you awake?"

I opened the door, and there he stood in his robe and slippers. He said, "We haven't spoken a half-dozen words since the crusade began, and I just wondered how you were." I told him I was OK and asked him to come in.

We must have talked an hour and a half before that conversation was over. I confided that maybe everything wasn't quite as "OK" as I led everybody to believe. I told him about the workload I carried and my driving obsession to do more and more. I confessed that I never spent any time with Vangie or Carol and told him how Carol was growing up under the same roof with me but I hardly saw her from day to day, how my relationship with Vangie was more like competitive brother and sister than husband and wife. I said that the panic of fighting deadlines deadened my guilt over being an absentee father and blotted out the loneliness of being a distant husband.

Dr. Bob said that he understood what I was feeling because many times his work had come between him and his family. He told me not to minimize the problem, because it could be the weak link in my armor and keep me from realizing God's best in my life. And then he prayed. I couldn't believe the quality of that prayer. Here was a guy that most of the time I was about half-afraid of, and for all his bluster and abrasiveness, and with a mountain of problems of his own, he was praying for me.

The Osaka Crusade was a great experience for me. I was on a team— a team doing kingdom business—and God was using the music we were making to bless people and bring glory to His name. My heart was glad for that. But down in one little corner it was sad, too. Oh, it was good to get home! I arrived with a determination to spend more time with Carol and Vangie. I wanted to bring my life back into balance, do more things together, maybe not work so hard.

But do you know, I wasn't home a week until I was back in the old rut again. Besides, Carol had stopped dropping into my little workroom after school to "bother me." In fact, she seldom came home after school. Vangie's own work schedule grew more and more demanding. She was doing recording sessions, TV, and film calls with some of the finest groups in the business. So despite my determination to change, things went quickly back to abnormal.

About this time, the music business was undergoing a very unfortunate change. At least I thought so at the time. There was this thing called "rock music" that all the kids were listening to. I'd go out to get into my car, and the radio would be set on a rock station. Guess who had done it? It really bugged me when Carol would spend her allowance on a "rock" record.

Even among the studio musicians, feelings ran high about this new kind of music, and if word got out that one of the "good" musicians had defected to the "rock camp," his demise was lamented with a grimace and a clicking tongue. I left no doubt in Carol's mind what I thought about "her" music.

Then one day Roger Williams called and asked if I could write a "rock" record for him. I paused to size up what effect my answer would have on my bread and butter. Then I said, "Why sure, Rog, no problem." A few days later we recorded *Born Free*.

Now today, that record would not, by any stretch of the imagination, be considered "rock and roll." But in the early 1960s, the addition of Fender bass and electric guitar, with the drums playing even eighth notes, got it an enormous amount of airplay on all the rock stations, and soon *Born Free* was a hit. (It won a Grammy!) And one afternoon Carol did drop by my office to ask if I was the same Ralph Carmichael that did *Born Free,* that was now being played on her station.

By now Vangie and I had a business manager and a full-time maid. "If you are successful, you should act like it" was the rationale. I was buying tailor-made suits from Sy Devore's, and to Vangie's growing wardrobe was added a fur. Our home in Encino was beautifully decorated and expensively furnished. Our cars were big and new. I even hired a press agent to keep my name in print. But it seemed that the harder I worked, the less we had, and the more that came in, the more we spent.

I got a call from Jimmy Baker and Jack Haley, Jr. who were producing the annual Thalian's Ball for Debbie Reynolds. "Would you be music director for the show?" It was a benefit to raise money for the Children's Hospital and was attended by almost everyone in the entertainment industry. The cause was noble enough, and "think of all the new contacts you'll make."

I said yes, provided I could have the band I wanted. Jimmy Baker was a band buff to begin with, so he said to get the best. I called my old friend, Hy Lesnick, who did my contracting, and he hired all the good studio musicians. That first year was an exciting show. The band really roared on the overture. Also, I had gotten very adept at taking bows. The highlight of the evening was when the guests of honor arrived late, walking down the center aisle of the grand ballroom in the old Beverly Hilton Hotel. That was my cue to strike up "Mr. Wonderful," and here they came—Liz Taylor and Richard Burton.

When Dr. Bob Pierce invited me to go back to Japan for another crusade, I was ready this time. He planned to go to Tokyo and had booked the great To-Ko-Kai arena, which seated twenty-five thousand people, for one solid month. The plan was to rehearse six thousand voices. We would use a different thousand each night on Monday through Saturday. Then Sunday would be volunteer night, and any of the six thousand could come.

Ells Culver had arranged to hire an eighty-six-piece symphony made up of members of three of the top orchestras in Japan—the NHK staff orchestra, the Imperial Symphony, and the Tokyo Symphony. It was a fine orchestra.

I picked the favorite arrangements from the Osaka repertoire and then added a lot of new ones. We needed music for thirty nights, and that's a lot of notes. We had some fine soloists: Gary Moore, Fague Springmann, Norman Nelson, Jimmy McDonald. And we had some fine keyboards: Charlie Magnuson, Loren Whitney, Kurt Kaiser. We also took my good friend, Jack Connor, to play mallets.

The choral music went to Japan months in advance and was published in a book with a shiny red cover and bold letters across the front: *TOKYO CRUSADE CHOIR.* Inside the book they had stripped in the Japanese lyrics over my English lyrics on all the arrangements except *The Hallelujah Chorus.* (You should have heard them try to pronounce those English lyrics—"How-ray-roo-ya." But oh, how they sang—my pulse quickens just to write it!) I brought the orchestra music with me in two large trunks—over ten thousand pages of parts, plus the scores.

At Dr. Bob's suggestion, Vangie and Carol were to join me after rehearsals were in progress, and expectations ran high for the great adventure that lay ahead. We had a very attractive suite at the New Japan Hotel, and I was very proud when my family arrived. I introduced them to the oriental sights as time permitted.

About her second day in Tokyo, Carol popped out with some very suspicious-looking dots across her forehead, her cheeks, and the bridge of her nose. From a distance it looked like a funny case of the freckles, but it turned out to be the saddest case of chicken pox any little girl could ever have. Now, Japan has very strict laws about contagious diseases, and they enforce them. No matter who you are or whom you know, if you have chicken pox, it's straight to the "pest house." That's what they call it, and that's what it is.

I had made the acquaintance of a World Vision missionary by the name of Nick Nickelson, who had ministered in the Tokyo area for some time. I found him now in the hotel lobby and told him what had happened. He scratched his beard, and his forehead furrowed with concern, but he said, "There is nothing that can be done. If the authorities find out, Carol will have to go to the pest house until she recovers."

If it had been me going to the pest house, I would have let him off the hook and accepted my fate. But Carol . . . ! I just stared at him, and the silence was awkward. Finally he said, "Wait here, I'll be right back."

He came back grinning. Ten minutes later, we were crowded into Nick's tiny car, headed for an unknown destination. He explained, while dodging through Tokyo traffic. A few miles outside of Tokyo was a Catholic convent, complete with hospital, and Nick knew the Mother Superior. While she was a very compassionate woman, she was also a great enforcer of rules and regulations and would not even consider checking Carol into the hospital for fear of the obvious consequences.

However, she had told Nick to come on out because she had a plan. Soon Nick pulled out of traffic, cut his speed, and entered a driveway through iron gates. We drove past a cluster of somber-looking buildings and on back to a rather new, four-story, cement-and-steel building with a high flagpole in front. But we didn't stop or pause; we went on past, leaving the asphalt and taking a rutted dirt lane back behind the new building. There we saw an old, dilapidated, two-story building that butted up to the new, four-story building at right angles. It looked like a candidate for demolition.

Nick stopped the car as the dust swirled around us. He said we were to wait. In a minute or so, two ladies in starchy uniforms came from a back door of the new building. One was short and oriental; the other was tall, wearing a dark shawl. Nick greeted the tall one in English and the short one in Japanese, which he spoke fluently.

We all got out of the car and followed the women toward the dilapidated old building. We walked up a flight of stairs and down a long, wide hallway, the flooring of which had been torn up, exposing the bare-board subflooring. There were sawhorses and debris scattered here and there.

At the far end of the hall was a little room that had been swept and dusted. There was bedding on a very narrow, single bed, and there was a sink, but no running water or electricity. We learned that the building was, in fact, going to be torn down completely later that summer and replaced with a new wing. But for now, it would be Carol's home until she got well. The only human contact would be the little Japanese nurse to bring her meals and tend to her needs.

The nurse spoke not one word of English, but she smiled. Vangie and I could visit Carol for short periods daily, sneaking in the back way. As we left, Vangie slipped a little Japanese/English dictionary into her hand, and we both kissed her. Later I cried; it was the first time since Dad died.

I will remember the Tokyo Crusade as one of the finest times of my life. By coincidence, Nat King Cole was doing a concert in Tokyo at the same time we were there. I made contact with his "roadie," who set up a brief meeting at the hotel. Nat looked great and seemed happy and relaxed. He said, "Raff, what in the world are you doing in Tokyo?" I told him about the Tokyo Crusade for Dr. Bob and World Vision and my symphony and one thousand voices for thirty nights.

He said, "I'll bet you're like a mad dog in a meat house. I've got an idea for an album when we get back, but you probably won't be interested after what you've had here in Tokyo." I said, "Try me." We laughed, shook hands, and said we'd see each other back in Hollywood.

Some years before, at Temple Baptist Church, I had written a little invitation song called, "The Savior Is Waiting." Dr. Bob loved that little song, so he had me do an arrangement of it for Tokyo. I used one of the soloists on the verse, with the choir "oohing" and the strings doing goose eggs (whole notes). Then on the bridge, where the lyrics are, "Time after time He has waited before," the whole thousand voices came in on the Japanese lyric, with all eighty-six musicians supporting. It was the thrill of a lifetime. (Maybe Nat was right.)

After the first night, Dr. Bob had us do "The Savior Is Waiting" each night at the close of his sermon for the rest of the crusade. Before that year was over, that little song had spread all over the world. During the month of the crusade, literally hundreds of Christian lay people and pastors who visited Tokyo carried that song back with them and introduced it to their congregations.

I had brought Irv Wright, my copyist, with me to Tokyo because in my spare time I was writing the arrangements for my first *102 Strings* album, which was scheduled to record after the close of the crusade.

The momentum of the crusade increased nightly. What was happening there in Tokyo was big news back in the States, as great throngs of Japanese people crowded to the front of the arena, clogging the aisles to accept Christ as Savior night after night.

You would not believe the organizational perfection of the choir. Each night there was a seating chart showing a thousand spaces. In each space, neatly calligraphed, was a Japanese name. At half-past six every evening, every choir member for that night was in the proper seat and ready for the prayer which preceded rehearsal. Even the orchestra members who were non-Christians reverently bowed their heads out of deference.

On the last night, which was Sunday, the choir seating was thrown open so that as many of the six thousand members as desired could participate on this closing night. The side balconies were marked off for extra seating, and besides the thousand singers on stage, we had an additional two thousand on each side, for an estimated total of about five thousand members. Dr. Bob allocated extra time that evening for the musical package, and we sang several of the selections that had become favorites during the crusade. I must have lost ten pounds that evening conducting that "monster" choir and orchestra.

Carol had finally lost her spots, along with any interest she might have had in Japan, and I saw Vangie and her to the airport for their flight home. I stayed to record the album.

To this day I get excited prior to a recording session. I guess it's a combination of delight and uncertainty. You approach each session absolutely positive that it will be the best yet; on the other hand, you're not quite 100 percent sure. It doesn't make any sense, does it? But the adrenalin flows every time.

This time in Tokyo was extra special. Of all the hundreds of sessions before, I'd never done one quite like this. We used the best strings from all three orchestras: fifty violins, sixteen violas, sixteen cellos, twelve Arco bass, four rhythm, two harps, and two percussion, for a total of one hundred two players.

My interpreter, whom I called Sen Se,* stood by my side throughout the whole session. He was a music professor at a local college and had worked with me throughout the whole crusade. I would have been lost without him.

The orchestra was set up on a large stage in one of the downtown auditoriums, and we were recording with the finest remote equipment money could buy, with lots of Telefunken microphones hanging overhead on giant booms.

During the second hour of recording, I noticed an empty chair over in the cello section, and I asked Sen Se about it. He just shrugged,

---

* A term of respect meaning "teacher" or "professor."

and we went on. But I was a little upset, because if I was paying for one hundred two players, I wanted one hundred two players.

Pretty soon, I noticed another empty chair over in the violin section. Glancing back at the cello section, I saw that the first vacancy had been filled. After a few minutes the empty chair in the violin section was filled. But now I had a vacancy in the viola section.

This continued until the annoyance was more than I could endure. I stopped the music and said, "Sen Se, what's going on here?" He was very embarrassed. Putting his face right up to my ear, he whispered, "Please sir, I am so sorry, but there is only one small toilet backstage, and you have so many musicians."

Throughout my musical career, I had wanted an orchestra this big. But I had never thought of that particular drawback! So some of the pieces on the *102 Strings* album really have only one hundred one strings. If you want a refund, let me know.

twelve

NEW AND DYING DREAMS

I returned home to troubled domestic waters but escaped the confrontations by throwing myself back into my work. For the first time in my life I found that I needed to write for money. Let's face it—we were living too high on the hog. Taxes were stacking up, and the double-talk from my business manager made no sense at all to me.

I began to stay in my part of the house and work while Vangie kept things going in the main part of the house. Very few people really knew what was going on, but our home situation was killing us both, with Carol caught right smack-dab in the middle. We were living a lie.

I'm stubborn and I'm stoic, so in the wee hours of the morning I'd have "think sessions" about our family life. I knew a lot of people who had less-than-perfect marriages, but they just made the best of it. Why couldn't I? After all, I really didn't have any options. In the evangelical vocabulary, the word *divorce* did not exist. I finally figured that if my work had gotten me into this spot, why couldn't it get me out now? So I'd pray my little, "Dear Lord, help me now" prayer and go back to work.

I would not be truthful if I denied that there were indiscretions. I was unhappy and lonely, visible and vulnerable. But the indiscretions were a symptom, not a cause. I had not been a husband for a long time. Vangie was beautiful and the best alto in town. Sure, I was proud of her. We kept up a good appearance in public. But music, the very thing that had brought us together, now was tearing us apart. Vangie was going her way and I was going mine.

No, I hadn't backslidden, and no, I hadn't turned my back on God. The problem was that God and I had switched roles. I was the pilot; He was the passenger. I was the leader; He was the follower. But follow me He did . . . even into the pit of despair. The tougher things got (and they would get tougher yet), the closer I felt to Him.

One evening Vangie said, "I want to talk to you." She had been crying. And what she had to say was short and sweet: "I want you to move out." The next day I did.

In order not to lose any time on my two current writing assignments, I found a cheap motel down on Ventura Boulevard near Van Nuys. The proprietor, whom I had never laid eyes on before, turned out to be an ex-trombonist in the Russ Morgan band. I told him my situation, and he said he had just the ticket for me—a cabin with a garage on one side and a deaf tenant on the other side. "See, it'll be perfect. You can write all night long without disturbing anybody."

Actually, he was happier about the whole idea than I was. But I moved my clothes, my piano, and an overstuffed Naugahyde chair into the motel. My room was about twelve-by-twelve feet, with three little adjoining cubicles—a closet, a half-bath, and a tiny kitchen. Do you know how much room you have left over in a twelve-by-twelve-foot space after you put in a bed, a chest, a piano, and an overstuffed chair? None!

I lived in that room for one year and wrote incessantly. It wasn't fun anymore; it was pure survival. My moving out of the house did not stop the bills. I still had to take care of Vangie and Carol—I *wanted* to take care of them. In addition, there were old debts, including restaurant bills and back taxes.

One night I called my friend, Hy Lesnick, whom I had met years before when I first started to work on sessions at Capitol Records. In the beginning, he had been just a contractor—hiring the musicians for the band, turning in the union reports, and preparing payroll information. But Hy was not like other contractors around town, many of whom were loud, power-hungry, and politically ruthless. Hy and Tootie, his wife, had become very close and supportive friends to both Vangie and me. Recently, in our difficult times, they had proved very sensitive to our hurts.

Usually when Hy got a call from me, it was to schedule some recording sessions. Tonight I had something else on my mind. I said, "Hy, I sit here and write all the time. Checks come in the mail or stack up at the Musicians Union. But the bills also keep piling up and don't get paid, and I don't know where I stand. Everything is just pressing in on me. Would you be sort of my business manager until I can get myself straightened out?"

Hy hemmed and hawed for a couple of minutes and said he'd never done anything like that before. But then he said that if I thought he could do it, he'd take a shot at it.

The next day he went with me to a very fine restaurant called The Tahitian, down the street from my motel. We had a talk with the manager, whose name was Bill Dove. You see, I owed a tab of about eight hundred dollars, and I couldn't pay it right then. What's more, I still had to eat a couple of times a day. So Hy told Bill that if I could still sign for my meals, we would keep current on a monthly basis, plus pay fifty dollars a month on the old debt.

I'll never forget the look on that guy's face. He said, "I don't believe it! You mean you can't pay your bill, and you're asking me to let you have more credit?" He wasn't angry, just nonplused. In fact, he thought it was funny enough to laugh about. Then Hy told him a little of my problem and said he would be responsible for getting the check to the restaurant on a regular and timely basis. Bill finally calmed down and said, sure, he'd be glad to help.

Well, old Hy was a real godsend. He held off the creditors, got me a tax accountant, arranged payout schedules on old debts, collected the money I was making, and paid the bills in a prudent and punctual fashion.

One day I was facing a particularly difficult financial crisis, and was shopping around in my mind for a way out, when I suddenly remembered some old master tapes I had stored away at Capitol. They featured a choir singing some hymns—nothing fancy; just good, middle-of-the-road material, right out of the hymnal. A couple of years before, I had met a guy by the name of Jarrell McCracken, who owned a record company back in Texas. He was a nice person, and his company was really doing well. In fact, I had worked for him a few times, although I had gotten the feeling that he didn't completely approve of what I stood for musically. But these tapes would be right up his alley—no rhythm, no brass, no strings . . . just singing.

I called him. And during the conversation he said, "What would I do with your tape?"

I said, "Release it as a new album."

He was not sure. "How do I know it would sell?"

I reassured him: "Call it the Ralph Carmichael Choir."

After a pause he said, "I'm not sure if that would help sell it or keep it from selling." And then he chuckled—that wonderful chuckle of his, which is really more musical than his singing. And he said, "OK, Carmichael, your check will be in the mail."

Two days later, the check arrived with a cover letter explaining that, due to the personal problems I'd been having, I would have to sign "the enclosed release" and return it to him, and that he was sure I would understand. Then I read the release. It said in effect that he would be able to release my tapes without using my name.

There it was. He had not been kidding.

Oh sure, I signed the release and cashed the check. But I also did a lot of thinking during the next few days. Had I actually sunk so low that nobody wanted to use my name on an album? I got mad, I got hurt, I got mean, and I got embarrassed—all at the same time.

I don't think I was mad at McCracken; that would have been like killing the messenger because he delivered bad news. I figured that Jarrell was just reflecting the attitude of the Christian public as a whole. He had his ear to the ground and had found out what people were feeling and thinking before the news got to me. But when I had to sign that release, I got the message all in one dose.

Now I really withdrew. There were only about three people in the world who knew where I was, and that was a secure feeling. I was cranking out more notes than Irv Wright could handle, so he found me another copyist by the name of Max Walter, who was really fast and didn't drink. (Irv had started drinking because of the pressure.) Those two guys, plus Hy and Tootie, were the only ones who could find me.

During the next twelve months, I averaged about one secular album a month, plus some TV and several films—no gospel albums. Not that I wouldn't have wanted to record a gospel album; it's just that nobody called.

One of the TV pilots I did was for Rowan and Martin at ABC. It was absolutely one of the zaniest shows I had ever seen. I guess it was too zany, because ABC never put it on the air. The following season it surfaced on NBC as *Rowan and Martin's Laugh-In,* but with another music director . . . oh well.

God bless Dick Ross. Through him, I continued to write for Bob Pierce at World Vision and for Billy Graham and Cliff Barrows at World Wide Pictures.

About that time, I began to write another kind of music. Remember, when you are in the music business, you only write when you have to—which is generally all the time. You write on assignment, and if you don't have a deadline, you don't write. You use those hours or that day to heal up, to recover from your last panic.

But now, in the middle of the night, I would find my mind wandering from the work at hand. And I would lay aside what I was doing and think; you might even have called it pondering or meditating. I'd even talk to God some. It wasn't really praying in a structured sense. I didn't make requests, and I didn't worship. I would just become acutely aware of His presence. I would review my messed-up life and sort of talk over with Him how I got to where I was, where we were going from here, and how would we get to where we were going.

Sometimes, right in the middle of one of those quiet sessions, I'd get an idea for a song. I can't remember all the songs I wrote during this period of time, but one of them was "Like a Lamb Who Needs the Shepherd"*:

> Where He leads me I must follow,
> Without Him I'd lose my way.
> I will see a bright tomorrow
> If I follow Him today.
> Like a lamb who needs the Shepherd,
> At His side I'll always stay.
> Through the night His strength I'll borrow,
> Then I'll see another day.
>
> Life is like a winding pathway;
> Who can tell what lies ahead?
> Will it lead to shady pastures
> Or to wilderness instead?
> Like a lamb who needs the Shepherd,
> When into the night I go,
> Help me find the path that's narrow
> While I travel here below.
>
> Though you walk through darkest valleys
> And the sky is cold and gray,
> Though you climb the steepest mountains,
> He will never let you stray.
> Like a lamb who needs the Shepherd,
> By your side He'll always stay,
> Till the end of life's long journey,
> He will lead you all the way.

I had moved into the motel cabin with the idea of staying a couple of weeks until I finished the album project I was working on. Now my stay was stretching on to almost a year. I had made a lot of money, paid a lot of bills, and done a lot of thinking about how to get my dreams back on the right track. The place had been good to me and had served its purpose, but now I started to get cabin fever.

During the rainy season I would get cold at night, so I'd turn on the wall heater, which was about two feet away from the piano bench. Within fifteen minutes my left side would be scorching, so I'd turn it off, and within another fifteen minutes I would be miserably cold.

I knew I didn't want to go through another winter in that little shack. And I also knew that God had something more in mind for my life than what I was doing. I remembered the deal I had made with God over fifteen years before. I also remembered the applied determination with which I had pursued my early dreams. And now some other dreams were beginning to form.

Do you know what I'd do back then? I'd look at my work and say:

Here's what God has given me to do.

Here's what God wants me to do.

Here's what I can do best.

Here's what I like to do.

So . . . here's what I'm going to do.

Then I would look at myself in the mirror and say:

Here's the way God has made me.

Here's what God wants me to be.

Here's what I want to be.

So . . . here's what I'm going to be.

Then I would think about that all the time.

I'd pray about it when I prayed.

I'd dream about it when I dreamed.

I'd work toward it when I worked.

I'd talk about it when I talked.

I'd make an effort to learn only things that would help me do and be these things.

I had these faith images that ordered my priorities during all my waking hours, and though I don't understand it all, I'm sure that the wheels of my subconscious kept turning even when I slept.

I knew there was a big force inside me—a big power system. But what good was it doing? Was it going to be destructive or constructive? When I had started out, the whole idea had been to use my music to communicate the gospel. But maybe I had gotten to the point that the music was using me.

Was it possible that there were one or maybe two things even more important than music? If that was so, I'd better find out pretty soon. What good was all I had learned? How could I accomplish all that I felt God wanted and expected from me if I had no credibility? Who would believe or trust me if I stayed invisible?

I knew God was doing something in my life. Still, to most people, I was just a pop music arranger separated from his wife. I had to hold steady and stay rational, to wait on God and see what He wanted from me.

Then I began to ponder again on the notion that what I *was* might be more important to God than what I could *do.* With a grin, I thought of a line from an old Sunday school song: "He'll never make you go against your will; He'll just make you willing to go!"

I knew that God had given music to His church. I had seen music provide blessing and inspiration to the believer. I had also seen music used to communicate the gospel to the nonbeliever. And, in an obscure way, I had even been a part of all this, having arranged and recorded for practically every Christian artist that ever cut a record. But I also knew what I had done was not enough. There was more—much more.

In recent months, the songs I had written were about discouragement, loneliness, heartbreak, fear, guilt, and disappointment. And believe me, I knew what I was writing about. I had been there and was living through all of those things. But I was also coming to know more than ever that God's *love* knows no bounds, His *mercy* endureth forever, His *grace* is sufficient, and His *joy* is unspeakable. I had personally drunk the cool, refreshing, "living water" from every one of these wells of salvation. The lyrics came from my own experience.

Gradually, the idea of sharing my songs with other people became exciting and even important. Oh sure, I was still very particular about the melodies and the chords, but I began to see that the message was the important thing.

I took seven of my songs and flew to Waco, Texas, to talk to Jarrell McCracken about a wild idea: "Jarrell, let's start a new music publishing company. We'll go 50-50; I'll write the music, you'll sell it."

Now, being a true businessman, Jarrell doesn't get too thrilled about just 50 percent of anything, and it was an uphill battle trying to interest him in going into business with me.

At first he said he'd have to think on it awhile. I told him I didn't have awhile and that I had some other interested parties.

He said, "Why don't you just assign the songs to Word, and we'll publish them?" I told him that I had put songs with other publishers before and that nothing ever happened to them. Once in a while, one would appear in sheet-music form with a plain cover. But I wanted more than that; I wanted to write some different kinds of music and to participate in the development of the copyrights. "I wanted you to have first refusal, but if you're not interested, no problem."

Well, we sparred around like that until after lunch, and he finally said, "OK, let's go over to the attorney's office." When we got there, I met Rodney Lee, the lawyer for Word. His Texas drawl was so heavy I could hardly understand him. He and McCracken were knocking some big words around, but when he said something about 51 percent and 49 percent, I understood that all right and didn't care for it a whole lot. But it seemed pretty important to them.

We argued a little while. I saw we were not getting anywhere, so I decided to show them that 50-50 was just as important to me as 51-49 was to them, and I headed for the door. I got my hand on the knob, but before I turned it we had a deal: 50-50. (Truthfully, Jarrell would have been worth that extra 1 percent. He's the best businessman in the world, and I do believe he could have sold horses to the cliff dwellers.)

Jarrell then said, "When you start a company, it's customary to put some dollars in for capital to get the thing off the ground." I had invested up to the hilt just to buy my plane ticket to Waco. So I said, "Silver and gold have I none, but I brought these seven songs with me, and I figure they are worth at least a thousand dollars. What are you willing to put in?"

He said, "Do you remember those forty-eight piano lessons you sold me for a thousand dollars a couple of years back?* If they are still worth a thousand dollars, I'll put them in the pot." So, we were capitalized at two thousand very soft dollars. I headed home as half-owner of Lexicon Music, Inc.—and president to boot!

Now everyone knows it's not fitting for the president of a corporation to live in a motel, so I moved forthwith. My new home was a small, five-room, one-story, frame house with a hedge around the front yard and a garage in which to store my music. There were about eleven hundred square feet under the roof, and it was furnished in "early odds and ends," but it was a castle compared to the motel. There

* Years earlier, I had put together a mail-order publication called *The Ralph Carmichael School of Music* and had sold it to Jarrell.

was a glass-topped table in the dining room which could easily accommodate two copyists, and on occasion I could set up a couple of borrowed card tables in the living room for two extra copyists, so they could all work through the night prior to a session. There was also a breezeway—a small patio that had been made into a room that had a sliding glass door added. That's where I set up shop with my piano.

Let the deadlines come . . . I was ready for anything. And come they did. I felt like a soldier in Nehemiah's army. Remember how he had his soldiers build with one hand and fight with the other? That's exactly what I was doing. With one hand I was trying to build Lexicon—writing songs and getting artists to record them. And with the other hand I was fighting for survival—writing arrangements to make a living.

As a bachelor, my housekeeping habits left something to be desired. I had just recorded with a gospel singer named Jack Holcomb and had invited him to come by and see my new pad. I never did bother to lock the front door when I left the house, so I wasn't too surprised to hear singing coming from inside as I pulled in from a show I was doing at NBC. And when I recognized the song as "Ship Ahoy," (his "sugar stick") I knew my visitor was Holcomb. What did surprise me was that he was standing in the kitchen with his sleeves rolled up and his tie tucked inside his shirt, washing a ten-day backlog of dirty dishes.

I said, "Jack, what in the world are you doing?"

He said, "What's it look like? Why son, a body could catch typhoid in this kitchen."

Hy Lesnick was still trying his best to keep my bookkeeping in better shape than my housekeeping. But he constantly pleaded for a little cooperation.

In the afternoon the postman would drop the mail through a slot in the front door, and it would pile up on the floor. Periodically I would pick it up and throw it on the divan, and there it would collect, unopened, until some more convenient time during the week or month.

I hardly noticed that one day there were several envelopes similar in appearance—sort of a strange yellow color. I did notice that there were several more the next day, and I just threw them on the couch with the rest. By the end of the week, I was pretty disgusted with all the strange yellow junk mail I was receiving, but it kept arriving.

The following week Hy Lesnick paid me a visit and asked if I had any mail that he should process. I said, "I think it's mostly junk mail" as I pointed to the couch. His jaw fell open, and he said, "Do you know what's in your so-called junk mail? Those are royalty checks from the Musicians Union Trust Fund. They've been in litigation for five years, and we've all been getting our settlement checks."

Tallied up, my strange yellow envelopes contained about eight thousand dollars. The money came in handy.

One day I picked up a large, ominous-looking envelope, and before I could deposit it on the couch, the words "Attorney at Law" in the upper left-hand corner caught my eye. I tore open the flap and saw "Plaintiff, Evangeline Carmichael; Defendent, Ralph Carmichael."

The attorney's cover letter instructed me to call. I did immediately, and then went in to see him. I agreed to give Vangie everything the attorney had requested in exchange for one favor—no publicity. He said, "No problem." That was 23 March 1964.

A few weeks later Max Walters, one of my copyists, came to work on Monday and said, "Congratulations." He pulled out the Sunday *Los Angeles Times.* There on the front page of the second section was a three-by-five-inch picture of Vangie with a bold headline: "The Song Is Ended for the Carmichaels." The caption read, "She sings goodbye to husband."

The accompanying article led off with, "Songstress Evangeline Carmichael wins divorce settlement." Then it outlined the settlement in detail, including dollars and real estate and listing the grounds as "general cruelty." I had not hired an attorney. I had not gone to court. I hadn't even known the court date.

I took the paper and walked back into the bedroom to read it again, and I thought, "Congratulations, my foot!" I felt sorry for Vangie; I felt sorrier for Carol; and I was feeling a fair amount of pity for myself. What would people think? What would people say? And what would people do?

I worked the rest of the day and night in silence, and when I plopped down on the bed at daybreak, I had decided that I had no control over other people, only over me. So the important things were, "What will I think, what will I say, and what will I do?" I prayed my "Dear Lord, help us now" prayer, and especially included Vangie and Carol. Then, to the sound of birds chirping themselves awake, I fell asleep for a few hours.

A short time afterward, I got one of the most welcome phone calls I could have imagined. It was from Dick Ross, and he wanted me to do the music for a Billy Graham film called *The Restless Ones.* It was a story about teenagers and was the most honest presentation of human need and God's provision that I had seen in a film up to that time.

The film hit me especially hard, and at the end of my first viewing, I walked out of the screening room just as the lights came on. Down the hall, I stepped into the men's room to gain my composure. In the quiet I thought, "Dear Lord, help me write music to match this magnificent documentation of your love."

I had already lived through a music change in the secular field with Roger Williams. I had spent years learning to write pretty chords and voicings for strings, brass, and woodwinds. Then suddenly the new "kids'" music was influencing even the adult performers. And we were having to learn a whole new approach with records like *Born Free*.

As I went to work on *The Restless Ones,* I felt there was a change coming in the gospel field as well. I knew I had to do more than use violins for the "good guy" and oboe for the "bad guy." The music had to be as relevant as this film and its message.

In addition to the cues, I wrote three songs: "The Restless Ones," "The Numbers Song," and "He's Everything to Me." And I went into the studio with a Fender bass, a set of drums, two guitars, and a keyboard.

What I wrote did not set well at first; in fact, I thought for a while I might have to redo the music for the film. But then, as some of the younger generation viewed the first print of the picture and responded positively, attitudes began to change. The song, "He's Everything to Me," was soon picked up and sung by kids across the nation. At summer camps, youth rallies, and on campuses you'd hear that little song being sung wherever kids would congregate.*

It felt good to be on the World Wide Pictures team, even if I was just barely on it by reason of a musical contribution. To occasionally see Billy Graham, Cliff Barrows, Bev Shea, and Tedd Smith gave me a sense of worth about what I was doing. And to spend long hours during the creative process with Dick Ross and his assistant, Jim Collier, provided inspiration and therapy of which they were not even aware.

I'm sure no one around me realized it at the time, but *The Restless Ones* spoke to me with great impact. With a broken marriage and loss of communication with my daughter, Carol, I felt as if I were wearing a sandwich board with "I am a failure" written across both front and back. And I wanted to do something about it.

---

* Publisher's note: Today, "He's Everything to Me" is well on its way to becoming contemporary Christian classic. As this book goes to press, 3,351,012 copies have been printed by Lexicon Music alone—plus approximately 10,000,000 in other publications. It has been translated and published in at least twelve languages and recorded more than 250 times.

The next day I phoned Carol: "Hey Keops, let's go to lunch." (When she had first learned to talk, she had tried to say "Carol," but it had come out sounding like "Key-ops," so that had become her nickname.) She showed up at The Tahitian with scraggly hair, wearing old jeans and a man's sweatshirt, five sizes too big, with a giant footprint right across her chest. She still looked beautiful to me, but I could never tell her so—at least not right then.

That was a fabulous lunch. It wasn't what we ate; I don't even remember that. But what was said during that short time together absolutely revolutionized our relationship.

The gist of it was that I told her I didn't approve of her, and she told me she didn't approve of me. But then I said that I loved her, and she said she loved me. We sort of developed that theme for the next couple of hours. I told her she was hostile, rude, and lazy in school, so how could I approve of that? And she said that I had neglected her, taken her home away, and divorced her mother, so how could she approve of that? I said, "Do you still love me?" She said, "Do you still love me?"

When both answers turned out to be yes, we discovered that maybe love shouldn't be connected to approval. In other words, she didn't have to win my approval in order to have my love. And vice versa. If she did something of which I didn't approve, she didn't have to worry about my withdrawing my love. When we walked to the parking lot, I had my arm around her and she had hers around me. That hadn't happened in a long time.

In the coming months we saw each other more and more, and a funny thing developed. I noticed that we began to find little ways to please each other—perhaps without even realizing we were doing it. I was a father again, and it felt good. But I was still a bachelor, and that didn't feel so good.

It was true that I could come and go as I pleased, but there was no pleasure in it. It was true that I could write day and night without interruption, but when the writing was through there was no one to share it with. More than once I had pulled off the freeway and fallen asleep on the way home from the studio, and no one even missed me or cared (except the police, and they had a funny way of showing they cared!) For a while there I fancied myself in love with every waitress who poured me a cup of coffee.

thirteen

A GIRL NAMED MARVELLA

In the fall of 1964 I did a five-day-a-week game show at NBC called *What's the Name of That Song.* The emcee was Wink Martindale. I had a small band—maybe six or so musicians. The idea was that the band would play a tune and the contestants would try to name the song. Sometimes we would play the tune over and over, and the contestants would take the full time allotted until the buzzer went off, disqualifying them. Other times, the contestants would name the tunes as fast as we could play them. I've seen them guess the right titles in just two notes—it's uncanny.

The point is, we never knew how many songs we'd use up on one show. So the producers always made us have forty selections ready. That's two hundred starts (songs) a week. When you think in terms of six men times two hundred songs, you have twelve hundred pages of parts, plus two hundred scores!

The writing I could handle. It was a little band, and I'd never do more than sixteen bars with repeats. But the logistics of building each book for each musician for each show boggled my mind. The unused tunes from previous shows had to be sorted out for later use as dictated by the scriptwriter, and all the tunes had to be in order for the proper instrument and the proper day.

We did two shows on Thursday and three shows on Friday, and they would air Monday through Friday of the following week. The money was good, and I figured I could stand the pressure for one season if I had a librarian to take care of all the details.

Through Flo Price, with whom I had recorded, I had met a little gal named Mar—at least, that's what they called her. She was actually Flo's sister-in-law, and her real name was Marvella Grace. (You're right; it reminds you of something you've seen in the hymnbook, because that's where her daddy got the idea for her name.) She was divorced and had three kids, and she was struggling financially.

I offered Mar the job, and she took it. Early on, she let me know that she was leery of "wild musicians and their irresponsible ways," but she sure was a good librarian. And she helped me in other ways, too. One day when she came over, she said, "It keeps getting darker and darker in this house; what's going on?" It was an easy explanation. I would simply never turn the lights off, and one by one they would burn out. When I got down to one light, I'd count how many I needed. Then I would go out and buy the exact number of bulbs for replacements, and we'd have brightness again for a while.

Mar said that was not the way things should be, so from then on the lights were replaced as they went out from a large supply of bulbs now kept on hand. She also began to educate me in the fine art of flipping off switches.

That Thanksgiving, Chuck Ohman, who was and is an excellent trumpeter and minister of music at Calvary Baptist Church of Hazel Park, Michigan, invited me to participate in a great Thanksgiving Day concert at the Ford Auditorium in Detroit. I told him I'd come if he'd put an electric piano in my hotel room so I could write while I was there. He agreed, and I went. Mar, who was from Michigan, gave me her parents' telephone number in Battle Creek and made me promise to call.

It rained hard the night before I was to leave. That morning, Mar called and said, "Have you checked to see how the music in the garage came through the downpour?"

I said, "Hang on; I'll look." The rain was still coming down, so I made a dash for the side door of the garage. I opened it to find about three inches of water up around the cardboard boxes of unsorted music that covered the floor, wall to wall, and were piled one on top of the other about chin height.

It was a mess—and getting messier. Fifteen years of handwritten notes were going down the drain, so to speak. I went back to the phone and made my report, along with the observation that nothing could be done because I had to leave for the airport within the hour.

But two things happened within that hour. One was that I did leave for the airport. But before that, Mar arrived in a van that she had somehow borrowed or rented. Backing up to the garage, she took off her shoes, rolled up her jeans, and started loading boxes of music from their watery grave. The dry stuff went directly aboard; the wet and soggy stuff was carefully transferred into the house for special handling.

That's the last thing I saw before I headed for the airport. I don't know how many trips it took, but when I returned, my whole library was safely and dryly stored in another location. Thanks to Mar, there was absolutely no permanent damage.

In Detroit, I did make the phone call to Mar's parents, Rev. and Mrs. Don F. Price. Everyone called them Mom and Pop Price, so I did, too. Mom insisted that I come to their home for Thanksgiving dinner. But I explained that I'd be in rehearsal during the day on Thanksgiving for the concert that night. She solved that problem by saying they would celebrate the day before. And I could see that "no" was not an acceptable answer.

I hated to lose a day of writing because I was working on a project that would be recorded the following Monday, but the idea of a home-cooked turkey dinner with all the fixings was more than somewhat appealing. So I said yes and took the address. That was on Tuesday. I worked through the night, then slept a couple of hours and dressed for my Wednesday noon appointment with Mom and Pop.

At about nine o'clock in the morning, I called the depot to check on the train schedule, only to be told that the next train would get me to Battle Creek at about five o'clock that afternoon. I checked the airlines; there would be no flights until the next morning. Plainly, I was in a jam. After all the trouble the Prices had gone to on account of me, I would never live it down if I walked in late to that Thanksgiving dinner—let alone over five hours late.

I left the hotel and got into a cab: "Take me to Battle Creek."

The cabby said, "Is that a street or an avenue?"

I said, "That's a town in Michigan."

He said, "You mean you want to take a cab all the way to Battle Creek?"

It turned out that the cabby had a sister living in Battle Creek, and he said he'd visit her while I had dinner. We dickered back and forth a little and ended up with a figure of a hundred dollars for the round trip, and I handed him the address and said, "Let's go." It was a cold, windy day, so I just leaned back, wrapped my overcoat a little more tightly around me, and dozed off.

When I finally got to the Prices', they were all there. (All except Flo and her husband, Bob, Mar's oldest brother. They were still back in California and would become our best friends.) You couldn't have put another body around that table. In fact, you couldn't have gotten another person in the house! But it was cozy, and everyone talked at the same time, and the food was fantastic. I met Mar's older sister, Frances, and her husband, Walt, and their three kids. Walt pastored a church in a neighboring town. I also met Mar's younger brother, Burdette, and his wife, Theresa, and their three kids. Burdette was Pop's assistant pastor at The Family Altar Chapel and also helped Pop run his radio station, WDFP.

No sooner was dinner over than Walt, who is quite an all-around musician himself, insisted that I play the piano and show him some of the "hot chords" I used in arranging for the "famous artists." When I finally convinced him that I couldn't play, my stock with him dropped to about a penny a share.

About ten minutes to three, I noticed through the lacy white curtains that my cab had pulled up, and Pop noticed it too. He said, "You just dismiss the cab, and I'll take you wherever you have to go—the depot or airport, whichever."

Then I said, "Pop, that's the cab that brought me from Detroit, and he's waiting to take me back." All the conversation stopped, and I couldn't tell if they were all impressed or disgusted.

On the way back to Detroit, I reflected on the terrific time I'd had and how I'd met just about the finest family in the world. I sure wished I could have played the piano for Walt.

In the next few months, my work for various artists took me to Mexico City, New York City, the Bahamas, Puerto Rico, Las Vegas, Chicago, Miami Beach, San Francisco, Lake Tahoe, and Philadelphia. And everywhere I went, I would think of Mar. I could tell I was falling in love, because I couldn't wait to get home. But I resisted. It was crazy, it didn't make sense, and I was sure it could never work; God wouldn't let it work. (At least, that's what I had always been taught about remarriage after divorce.)

Finally I called my mother and told her I needed to talk to her. She had taken the loss of Dad very hard, but now she was her old self again and was busy with her Bible studies, counseling, and speaking engagements.

It wasn't easy to talk to Mom about my personal life, because she had always been very strict about certain matters. Things were either black or white—all right or all wrong. Here again that word *approval* popped up in my mind. I felt that I was a double disappointment to her. I hadn't made it as a preacher, and then I had capped the disappointment off with a broken marriage.

Still, Mom knew the Scriptures better than any human alive. She loved God, and I was sure she still loved me, so I was anxious to know what she felt and what she would say about my perplexing situation. We talked, and I told Mom all about Mar—about her folks, about her background and the problems she had gone through, but most of all about the fact that I loved her.

Mom usually had all the answers, but I could tell this was rough for her. Notwithstanding all the familiar passages on marriage and divorce, Mom found some verses that established God's law of equity (Ps. 98:9 and 99:4; Matt. 19:10–12). She said, "Son, I can't tell you what to do. I know that God is a reasonable God, and while He is just and demands obedience to His Word, He is also merciful, and He loves you and wants the best for your life. You are going to have to work this out for youself." Then she prayed a long and fervent prayer that I would find God's will and act on it.

As we parted, Mom said, "By the way, have you talked to Mar about marriage?" The fact is, that was one detail this old procrastinator hadn't taken care of as yet.

During the next few weeks, I tried the idea out on several of my close friends. Kurt Kaiser, with whom I had developed a deep friendship during the Tokyo World Vision crusade, said that if Mar would have me, I'd better jump at the chance. Jarrell McCracken hoped "She would bring some order to your chaotic life." Cy Jackson said, "She's just what the doctor ordered." So I finally popped the question to Mar, and she said yes.

The wedding date was set for October 28. We would be married in the wedding chapel at Highlands Inn in the picturesque little village of Carmel by the Sea.

You don't usually think of weddings as being fun, but ours was. I composed a telegram, and Mar thought it was grand. We sent it to some of our friends:

> There once was a girl named Marvella,
> Who loved this particular fella.
> Ralph was his name,
> Arranging his game,
> They got married today in Carmella.

When I married Mar, I automatically took on the responsibility of raising her three children. Any way you look at it, that's just not a logical thing to do. But love is not always logical. Mar as much as said, "Take me; take my kids."

I was willing to take them, but the question was, would they take me? In the months before our marriage, when I had first met the kids, I was willing to do anything to win them. I would have been a clown or a hero, bribed them or bragged on them—whatever was necessary to have them accept me.

One evening a few weeks after I had met Mar, she invited me to have dinner with her and the children. For months I had been eating canned goods or junk food, so the prospect of some home cooking was almost irresistible. I arrived sporting a close shave, a clean shirt, and an extra splash of cologne, but they were all to no avail. Mar was obviously embarrassed that I was getting the cold shoulder from all three kids.

Greg at age twelve, with his hair plastered down, had an extraordinarily deep voice. He played the role of man of the house. Andrea at age ten was the budding debutante. And Erin, aged six, was the clown princess. Mar's suggestions toward cordial hospitality were followed with painful reluctance, and everyone ate in silence, meditating on the flowered design that ran around the edge of the dinner plates.

The food was great, and the antisocial ambiance didn't affect anyone's appetite—there were no leftovers. As Mar cleared the table in preparation for dessert, I spotted a big lemon atop a bowl of fruit on the counter. It was a real lemon complete with the name *Sunkist* ® stamped in green ink.

Remembering an idiotic trick I had pulled a time or two in college to get attention, I reached for the lemon and announced to the kids that I preferred fresh fruit for dessert over what their mother was planning to serve. Greg looked wide-eyed and prepared to speak to me for the first time that evening. He said, "That's not fresh fruit; that's a lemon."

I said to Greg, "Could you eat that in one bite?"

The girls chimed in, "Oh, no, Greggie, don't do it; you'll choke."

And with that I popped the whole lemon in my mouth—rind, seeds, green ink, and all. It took a moment to get things adjusted, but after warding off the inclination to choke, I began the tortuous task of pulverizing my pungent mouthful. I remember thinking, "Did I really do this in college?"

Well, the expressions of disbelief on the faces of all three kids gradually turned to glee, and finally I was actually receiving cheers of encouragement. It took the better part of ten minutes before I was safely out of the woods and enjoying the congratulations, handshakes, and back-slaps, but that old lemon sure did the trick. Mar shot me a knowing grin and rewarded me with an extra big helping of homemade chocolate cake a la mode.

But there was a lot more to this matter of getting to know Mar's kids than just eating lemons. I had Carol tucked securely under my wing, and I didn't want anything to disturb that. But now I had to find a way to tuck three more under my other wing. And it didn't happen all at once. Just a loving step at a time.

After we were married, I returned to work in my bachelor house and Mar went back to the kids and her little home in Granada Hills—but not for long. By the following Sunday, she had found three places to show me, one of which might prove suitable as the new Carmichael residence.

The first appointment was shortly before sundown that Sunday. It was in Woodland Hills—a sprawling, one-story, shake-roofed dwelling that sat on a hill looking out over the San Fernando Valley, complete with pool and landscaping. The garage adjoining the kitchen had been converted into two small rooms that would be perfect for my work. We decided to look no further and went into escrow on Monday morning. By Thanksgiving we were all settled in. The only real furniture we had was Mar's antique oak dining-room table and beds all around. Because the oak table was for special occasions only, we ate off a picnic table in the kitchen, and we were happy.

Learning to be a father was more difficult than I can put into words. I am not and never have been a disciplinarian. In a studio with a choir and orchestra, I can be a tyrant, but as soon as the session is over, I step out of that role. With Carol, most of the discipline had been left to her mother or grandmother. Now I had the responsibility of caring for three more children, and that sometimes included laying down the law.

Mar said, "Now Ralph, you just have to do it." We set up some rules and regulations and did the best we knew how, a day at a time, to be consistent in meting out equal portions of love and discipline. Mar was a fantastic mother, and as the kids grew up, each one taking his or her turn at exasperating us, she would hang in there and never give up.

I wanted our kids to have a Christian commitment, but I could not force my theology on them any more than the president of the

United States could legislate worldwide peace. Minute by minute, a day at a time, I had to live Christianity in front of them when at times I felt more like knocking their heads together.

But of course there were rewards. One by one, the kids discovered what I did during those long work hours hidden away in the back of the house. And how pleased I would be when they would show some little sign of being proud of me. I'd think of how I responded to that, and then I'd find a way to show them that I was proud of them as well.

In the evenings, Mar and I would sit out by the pool and look over the Valley. First we'd watch the sunset, then we'd watch the lights of the Valley appear like a million acres of sparkling diamonds. I'd tell her what I had done that day and what I had to accomplish the next . . . what I dreamed of doing in the future. Even though she is the most practical person you've ever met, she was never surprised at my dreams. And while I worked, she worked beside me.

Her first project was sorting, cataloging, and filing my library. When the previous owners had remodeled the original garage, which was connected to the house, they had also constructed a separate, two-car garage at the edge of the property. Mar had a carpenter build in wall-to-ceiling cabinets on two sides of this structure so it would serve as a library as well as a place for cars. Everything I had written would be right at my fingertips, in my own garage, with an alphabetical card file and a reference number for immediate location. She has kept the library current through the years, and today I have more than three thousand arrangements and a hundred motion picture and TV scores.

Over the past year and a half I had written a number of songs, and Jarrell and I decided to use the royalties to publish our first music book. The first month's Lexicon sales were $76.33. Don't laugh. I had heard of the danger of growing too big, too fast, and we were doing all we could to avoid this pitfall.

In 1966, I went to McCracken with another brainstorm. I told him I wanted to record a different kind of album. He asked what would be different about it. I told him it would be kids' music with "even eighth notes" and a sort of "folk-rock" style.

Jarrell didn't know what I was talking about, but he never let on. He just asked what songs I would record. When I told him I wanted to use all my own pieces, he said, "Don't you think that's a bit presumptuous? What would you call it, *Carmichael Plays Carmichael?*"

I told him the record would be very low budget because I would only use about eight or ten musicians. I believe we called it *The Restless Ones,* and as Jarrell predicted it didn't sell—not right away, at least. But by Christmastime he had called me to ask if he could put it in the Word Record Club as a bonus offer. Since my record had already been out for six months, it would only qualify as a bonus record, which sold for a dollar, as opposed to the full price of a new release. Besides, he pointed out, he was taking some risk in giving the record exposure in the Record Club because of the potential criticism the record was bound to get.

I agreed to let him use the record, and was thankful for the opportunity to have more people hear this new kind of music. But that experience nudged me toward the development of an idea I had shared with Mar. I wanted to start a new record label in connection with Lexicon.

Through the years I had noticed a growing interest in the music I was doing on the part of choir directors and vocalists. People from the most unexpected places would find my address and write to request a copy of such and such an arrangement from such and such an album. Naturally, I was so flattered that I would find some way to run off copies and fill the request free of charge. I hoped that some day the demand would grow to such proportions that I would be able to compile books of these arrangements and offer them for wide distribution.

I also began to see the relationship between publishing and recording. If you recorded something that people liked to listen to, perhaps they would also like to buy the music and sing it as well.

I made another trip back to Waco to talk to Jarrell. I can't remember our conversation word for word, but I do recall saying that I felt a need to record gospel music at a new level of relevancy. I told Jarrell that, in my opinion, the evangelical status quo was stifling, even bordering on censorship, and was counterproductive to the whole concept of evangelism. We were more interested in producing music that pleased the ear of the older generation than in actually reaching out and communicating with the younger generation. And if something wasn't done to change the trend, the church would suffer for generations to come.

McCracken agreed but said, "What can we do?" Word had a very respected image. The records they produced were right down the middle—very conservative and dignified. It just would not do for them to start releasing contemporary kids' music.

I suggested that if we started a new label and released all the experimental music on it, then the Word label would not get the criticism.

Jarrell asked, "What would you call this new label?"

And I had a ready answer: "I'd like to call it Light Records."

"Why *Light?*"

"It just seems to me that *Light* and *Word* go together rather well, since both are symbols of truth and strongly biblical."

Jarrell wasn't that enthusiastic about the name, but he finally agreed. And I have to admit that sometimes the name was misunderstood. Occasionally someone would say, "Are you going to produce 'light-weight' records?" or, "Is your record company a division of 'lite beer'?" At any rate, the name stuck, and we had "Light Records, a Division of Lexicon Music, Inc." Now all we needed to do was record an album.

When I returned home, Mar said I had a call from Bufe Karraker, head of the Fresno Youth for Christ, and Larry Ballanger, his assistant. They were producing a film and needed some music. They also said they didn't have any money. I told them not to let that stand in the way. So they drove down to Los Angeles, and we had a meeting to discuss a plan for a "no budget" film score.

The idea was that I would write a title song for their film, and we would record both a vocal version and an instrumental version. Then we would lay one or the other of these tracks in appropriate places throughout the film. The story of the film had to do with a teenager's search for the answer to life, and the lead was played by a little gal from Fresno YFC named Rosemary Nachtigall. Rosy sang and played pretty fair folk-style guitar, and we decided that she would do the recording.

Bufe and Larry gave me a script, and I said I'd send them a song in a couple of days. I also made the rather cavalier offer to write a second song if they didn't like the first.

The first song I wrote and sent was entitled "Love Is Surrender," and you're right, they didn't like it: "*Surrender* is not a kids' word, and, in general, we don't think you've written a kids' song." I countered with the claim that the number-one song on the kids' chart at that time was a tune called "Cherish," and *surrender* was not dissimilar to *cherish,* but they still didn't buy it.

So I wrote song number two, which was called, "I Looked For Love." They liked it. Rosy learned it, and we set a date to go into the studio to record.

Then I got an enterprising idea. Why not record enough songs so that we could release an album? I told Bufe and Larry that the album would help promote the film, and vice versa. The long and short of it was that Light Records had its first release, featuring Rosemary Nachtigall: record #LS-5500, *The Searching Generation.*

But that's not quite all of the story. There was still the matter of having my number-one song turned down, which I said didn't matter at all. But on the inside, I felt rather bad about the rejection. I took my little "surrender" song and put it in the drawer. It was out of sight but not out of mind. Wouldn't it be great if a million people could hear the message of that song?

The late '60s and early '70s were the era of "youth musicals" such as *Tell It Like It Is* and *Natural High*. Writing with Kurt Kaiser, who lived half a continent away in Texas, created a hectic schedule, but the results were worth it—those were great days! *Left:* Kurt and I pose with Word Music marketing director Noni Wells over stacks of manuscript.

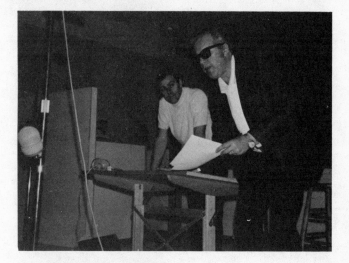

Above: In the recording studio. *Left:* Composers and choreographers coming up with a brilliant idea for *Natural High*. Left to right are Ralph Carmichael, Kurt Kaiser, Ellen and Alex Plasschaert.

Conducting choral workshops consumed a lot of time and energy during the 1970s. The shots on this page were taken during a MUSICalifornia workshop. When you've got a thousand choir directors in the audience, you'll do almost anything to sell them some music!

eading session at a workshop: They came to learn...

...and they came to sing.

Photos this page by Don Mazer Photography

Above: Kids can really pull the best out of a conductor. This shot was taken in the studio while recording the Gene Bartlett kids' compilation, *Paw Paw*. The part of Paw Paw was recorded by Thurl Ravenscroft, the famous voice of "Tony the Tiger." *Right:* The Jubilate Committee honored me with the Christian Achievement Award on New Year's Eve, 1980. The presentation was made by my long-time friend, Cy Jackson.

Dr. Bob Pierce, founder of World Vision, was one of
a kind. He provided funds and inspiration through
much of my early career.

This shot with my old friend, Dr. Billy Graham, and
his wife, Ruth, was taken on the set for the Billy
Graham Christmas Special, for which I arranged and
conducted the music.

In 1979 Jarrell McCracken, president of Word, Inc., visited our ranch, and we talked about my acquiring Word's half of Lexicon/Light. He also sold me a straight Egyptian Arabian mare.

My two best friends, my wife and my horse. (The horse is Farlo⁺, who was
National Reserve Champion in 1963. Farlo⁺ is now 28 years old, and we still
ride him regularly through the trails of the Santa Monica Mountains behind
our ranch.)

What a treat to have four generations in one photo! Left to right are my mom, Adele Carmichael; granddaughter Amanda; son-in-law Dean Parks; daughter Carol Parks; and me, holding the totally oblivious latest addition, granddaughter Acacia (1982 photo).

This photo of my stepson, Greg, and me was taken at a burro race in Big Bear, California, in 1982. Greg came in second place out of 63 entries.

This is my stepdaughter Andrea with her husband, Jeff Ellis, and their baby, Megan, in 1984.

Stepdaughter Erin was the last one out of the nest. This is her high-school graduation picture, taken in 1976.

Photo by White's Studios

Arabians aren't the only kind of horses we keep on our ranch in Hidden Valley. Here, Mar and I are having fun with two of our miniature horses.

In 1984 Mar and I traveled to Africa to help film a television special for World Concern.

In 1985 I had the honor of being elected to the Gospel Music Association Hall of Fame.

fourteen

GREAT IDEAS

One night I was sitting on the kitchen counter bothering Mar while she was trying to get dinner, and I told her I had a great idea. Do you know how many "great ideas" Mar has had to listen to? Well, enough so as to know how to do it in a very professional manner. But I felt very keen about this one and proceeded to describe it in detail.

We would publish a three-by-five-inch, pocket-sized, kids' chorus book. We would reduce the music to the simplest form possible—just a melody line and lyrics so kids could sing in unison and a chord symbol above the line so they could accompany themselves on guitar. The book would have a shiny red cover and would include fifty-three new and old kids' songs, plus the song I had written for *The Restless Ones,* "He's Everything to Me."

Mar said, "I suppose you'll call it, *He's Everything to Me Plus 53.*" And I said, "That's a great idea!" We did it. That little book was followed by *He's Everything to Me Plus 103.* Then came *He's Everything to Me Plus 153.* The accumulated sales were 1,278,562 copies.

The whole point of that story is to trace the travels of my poor little rejected song, "Love Is Surrender." Naturally, I included it in the first edition of our pocket-sized chorus book.

One day the phone rang, and on the other end was a lady from A & M Records' music clearance department. She wanted a license on a Lexicon tune they had just recorded. "Yes, that would be fine. What is the song title? . . . Oh yes, 'Love Is Surrender.'. . . And who recorded it? . . . The Carpenters? . . . How nice. . . ."

141

For those of you who don't remember, the Carpenters were an immensely popular brother-and-sister pop group in the late '60s and early '70s. It seems that Richard Carpenter had come across the little red chorus book at a youth gathering at his church and, leafing through, had found "Love Is Surrender." He and his sister, Karen, had recorded it, and now I couldn't wait to hear it.

When the Carpenters' album, *We've Only Just Begun,* was released, I rushed to get a copy, only to find that the lyrics had been changed. I studied the changes with a lump in my throat. If they had deleted the gospel message, it would cause a furor on the part of all the Christian kids who had learned to love that little song.

I listened over and over. It hadn't been changed to a "boy-girl" song, but the specific references to God's love had been omitted, and now it was just about "love." But then the thirteenth chapter of Corinthians was just about "love," too. And besides, what could I do now? The song was already recorded and released. What good would it do to sue? I decided just to sit tight and collect the royalties.

The album sold two million copies, and my royalty check was the largest check I'd ever seen up to that time. Instead of depositing it right away, I kept it in the top of my desk drawer.

About that time I received another call from Bufe and Larry. They needed to raise funds for Fresno YFC and wanted to talk to me. Two days later, in the office at the back of my house, we finalized plans for them to take one thousand albums at cost to sell in the Fresno area, with proceeds to go to YFC.

Throughout our meeting, I knew that just inches away in my top drawer was that royalty check from the sales of the song they had rejected. I don't know if the devil made me do it or if it was just old ornery Ralph rising to the surface, but just before they left I said, "How would you boys like to see something?" I'm not proud of it now, but I just had to rub their noses in it. So I pulled out the check.

In those early days of Lexicon/Light, every day and every night was packed with adventure. I'm going to have to leave out some of the exciting things that happened, but I will include a few that come to mind.

It seemed that I was writing new songs almost weekly—sometimes daily. I would either write them on assignment for a TV program or film or I would get an idea for a song from some personal experience. Perhaps the kids would be having questions or problems, and I would have had the same questions or problems before them, so I'd just write a song and share with them what I believed the Bible said on the subject.

I found that if a song was to endure, to be strong and effective, it had to be scriptural—absolutely had to be. I remembered hearing my first Billy Graham radio program called, *The Hour Of Decision.* The whole broadcast had been terrific—the announcer, the music, the continuity, everything. But when Billy had started to preach, and he'd shouted, "The Bible says," or "God says"—well, that was it. It was the most powerful statement anyone could make.

Oh, how I thanked God a thousand times over for the Bible I had learned growing up in the Carmichael household, with family altar every day and church almost every night. And even as I looked back on my frustrating years in Bible college, I could now see how valuable they had been in preparing me for the job God had given me to do.

At any rate, I used every opportunity possible to write songs. Even if there was no room in a film for a full-blown song, I'd make sure to include a few notes that could be turned into a theme and then expanded to thirty-two bars that would be suitable at a later date as the setting for a lyric.

The song, "I Found What I Wanted," was originally just an eight-bar theme used under the titles of a documentary of one of Billy Graham's campaigns called *The London Crusade.* Years later I expanded it and wrote the lyrics and got it recorded about fifty times.

The same thing happened in a film that Dick Ross produced with Billy Graham for the New York World's Fair. It was called, *Man in the Fifth Dimension.* In one of the music cues I had written, there was a little recognizable six- or eight-note theme. I later developed it into a complete melody and wrote a lyric called, "Beyond All Time."

As the songs piled up, I burned with the desire to get them recorded. What a thrill it was to get a call from Sam Wolgemuth, President of YFC International. They wanted a kids' album with a fresh sound and all new tunes. We would produce and pay for the album, but rumor had it that YFC International would buy about forty thousand copies wholesale and then resell them in cities all across the nation to raise funds for local rallies. What a break!

The year was 1968, and I went to work in high spirits. The songs included: "I Looked for Love," "A Quiet Place," "You Can Touch Him If You Try," "A Living Circle," "One of These Days," "Love Is Surrender," "I'm Gonna Go Back," "There Is More to Life," "The Ballad of St. Peter," and "Land without Tears."

I used eight singers and a rhythm section, plus a few other instruments for color. The cover was graphic art displaying some guitars, and the title song was "I Looked For Love." When the album was finished, we did in fact ship forty-four thousand copies to Youth for Christ.

There was just one sour note in this otherwise sweet experience. Although I thought the rhythms were really quite gentle, I guess they were not quite gentle enough. Within two weeks, more than four thousand records had been returned from local YFC directors around the country who found the album "quite objectionable."

But the best part of the story is yet to come. A couple of years later, we did another album for YFC. This time they also wanted a fresh sound and new material. In fact, I wrote most of the songs especially for the album. One of the tunes was "Our Front Porch," and they picked that for the title of the record. They shot the cover showing a group of young people of various nationalities sitting on a dilapidated front porch of an old frame house with weeds growing in the yard.

When the project was completed, we again shipped forty-four thousand records, and again a couple of weeks later about four thousand of them came back, probably from the same guys who had returned them before with the same explanation, "This record is too far out and is quite objectionable."

But here's the interesting part. The letters went on: "Please replace these objectionable records with the one you produced a couple of years ago called, *I Looked For Love*. We can really use that one." That experience was further proof that although change comes slowly, it does come.

From our first month of billings, which had amounted to about seventy-six dollars, we were growing by leaps and bounds. The only problem was that even though sales were up, profits were practically zilch. It wasn't that I wanted to put the profit into my pocket (in fact, I didn't take a salary in those days). But we needed money to fund the projects that were coming along.

I shared my concern with some of my close friends, and they suggested that I do some "cost analysis" (whatever that was!). At any rate, I did check into how much various books and records were costing us to manufacture; then I compared that figure to the amount we were selling the product for.

The big revelation came when I discovered we had one particular music book that retailed at a dollar and a half and cost fifty-one cents to print. We had a distribution contract with Word that essentially called for Lexicon/Light to receive one-third of the retail price for each unit sold. Since the one-third we received from Word on that book amounted to fifty cents, we were *losing* a penny for every book we sold! And the more product we sold, the more money we lost. We finally renegotiated our contract and arrived at a more equitable agreement.

One evening Kurt Kaiser, Director of Music at Word and a fine composer and pianist, was having dinner with Mar and me at our home in Woodland Hills. The phone rang, and I excused myself to answer it. The spirited voice on the other end belonged to Billy Ray Hearn, who at that time was with Word Records.

Billy Ray said, "Hey, I've got a great idea."

I said, "What's that?"

He said, "You and Kurt should write a kids' musical."

I said, "Well, Kurt just happens to be here. Let me get him on the extension." When Kurt got on the other phone, the three of us spent the next half-hour brainstorming the possibilities of what promised to be a most exciting project. That was the night *Tell It Like It Is* was born.

It was decided that Kurt would write half the songs, and I'd write the other half. During the following weeks and months, we commuted back and forth between Hollywood and Waco, Texas (Kurt's home), at least a dozen times. I got to be a regular customer on American Flight 134 that left Los Angeles about forty-five minutes after midnight to arrive in Dallas just before sunrise. I'd sit around the airport for an hour or so and then head for Waco by private plane.

Kurt and I would work all day. We'd show each other what we had written, talk about continuity, then perhaps decide to change the order and add a few more songs. When the day was over, we each had new writing assignments, and I'd head back to Dallas before sundown in the puddle-jumper to catch the night flight nonstop back to Los Angeles.

The drive home from the airport on those days was murder. I'd roll the windows down, blare the radio, slap my face, and sing anything that came to mind as loud as I could. I had some close calls, but I always made it, and I'm convinced I have the good Lord to thank for that.

From time to time, Kurt and I would meet with Billy Ray to show him the progress we were making and get his approval and encouragement. Sometimes he'd make constructive suggestions, or sometimes he'd just give us affirmation that we were on the right track.

When the writing was completed and all of the arrangements copied,

145

we recorded it in Ft. Worth, Texas. Then in early 1969, the albums and books were shipped to bookstores and music stores all over the United States and Canada.

Tell It Like It Is took off like wildfire. It was advertised as a "folk musical." I remember that during an interview with the religious editor of a local paper, I was asked, "What makes *Tell It Like It Is* a folk musical?"

The truth is, I was stumped, but without batting an eye or skipping a beat, I responded with all the authority I could generate: "*Tell It Like It Is* is a whole lot of music that we hope will be sung by a whole lot of folks."

I think that kids were ready for something they could call their own. Also, the churches were ready to try anything to get their youth mobilized again. Then the work itself, with all its artistic flaws, had some things going for it that really worked. The melodies were simple, the rhythms catchy, the lyrics were more or less in kids' vernacular. Most important, it was scriptural and Christocentric. It let the kids and the church get involved at the same time. They could sing and share the faith; they felt their worth again; it was like the church discovering a sleeping giant in their youth. The kids got a chance to unleash all of their pent-up energy, while the church got a chance to harness it and put it to use as a great witness throughout the community.

As hundreds, perhaps even thousands, of churches remobilized their youth to present *Tell It Like It Is,* the invitations for me to appear as "guest conductor" started pouring in. My first reaction was to say yes to everyone. After all, I had begun to think that life was one big rejection, and to suddenly be wanted and to have some approval was a very heady experience.

But flying back late one night after having conducted a presentation of *Tell It,* I was reflecting over the events of that day and evening. It had been an exciting experience. The choir, soloists, instrumentalists, lighting and sound crew, and the entire support team had been in preparation for weeks. The audience had been most enthusiastic, and the response when the invitation had been given during the singing of "Pass It On" was very moving. I thanked God for letting me be a part of this wonderful thing that was happening.

But then it occurred to me that the part I was playing might really be counterproductive. After all, the local director had done all the work. The evening was really the product of his or her vision and commitment. He or she was the one who had agonized through the long hours of rehearsal and had brought the kids along step by step in both physical and spiritual preparation. Then suddenly, three hours before the evening performance, I had arrived with all the accompanying hoopla as some sort of celebrity. After running through the music once, I had felt my way with a little caution and a lot of uncertainty through the presentation before a packed house, and I had walked away with the laurels and the congratulations.

I decided then and there to try a new idea. Thereafter, when I was invited to come and conduct a performance, I offered an alternative plan. I would come and be in attendance for the evening performance, but I would not conduct. Then I would suggest that the choir director put together a workshop during the day and invite other choir directors from that area to attend a reading session which I would conduct, and then they could stay over that evening for the presentation of the musical.

I insisted, however, that the local choir director conduct the evening performance. In some cases, it turned out that maybe I could have done a better job, but that would have robbed the local director of a very valuable experience. And so my new plan became a policy, and as much as possible, I made it stick.

Now that I've brought up the subject of workshops, I should tell you that my first few were very enlightening. The idea of calling the new form "folk music" didn't sit well with a lot of people. I thought the fact that one church in the area had discovered *Tell It Like It Is* meant everyone was accepting this new kind of music. I was soon to learn my error. In nearly every one of those first dozen workshops, someone would stand and, stimulated with the unction that accompanies the certainty that "right" was on his or her side, would call our new music "a tool of the devil." I was accused of bringing rock-and-roll music into the church with the ulterior motive of desecrating God's house and corrupting the young people.

That hurt—it really hurt. I would fly home with my tail between my legs and spend the next day staring out across the valley from the window of my study. The silence would attract Mar's attention, and she'd come in and ask me what was wrong. I'd say, "Oh, I'm just thinking," and I *was* thinking, I'll tell you that! I'm going to tell you some of the things I was thinking, because perhaps that will help you understand the decisions we've made at Lexicon/Light through the years.

I know now that it is not always good to have everything we do accepted with open arms by everyone. If that happened, we might get the idea that we could do no wrong, and that's just not true. Being exposed to criticism forces us to take stock, to examine our motives, to stand back and take a long look. We have to make sure we are right; we suddenly realize we can't take it for granted. We might even seek the comfort of a conference with God Almighty. Maybe the only time He can get His two cents' worth in is when criticism wilts our arrogance. So then, maybe this rejection thing is not all bad after all.

During my quiet times I thought about all these things, but I always came back to my first resolve. It seemed to me that most of the to-do about music was just a matter of personal taste.

I was hearing people say, "This music is bad" or "This music is evil" or "God can't use this kind of music." But did they really believe that? Or was it just that they didn't understand the music in question, and that people tend to fear what they don't understand and dislike what they fear? Were they just elevating their own taste in music by labeling it "godly" or "spiritual" while everything else was "worldly"?

I decided that I'd try my best to keep an open mind as new things came along and that I would not allow my personal tastes in music to limit the effectiveness of my ministry in music.

In those days, I also did a lot of thinking about how to make people aware of our products. I had heard of the tremendous sales volume of "door-to-door" industries such as Avon, Fuller Brush, and many more. It occurred to me that these were products that needed to be demonstrated or sampled; the customer had to feel the texture and smell the fragrance. Perhaps I could adopt some of these procedures to the marketing of our new music.

I decided that the only way to break down the barriers was to take the music directly to the choir directors and demonstrate it in front of them—to show them how it works, teach them the rhythmics, let them sing it and hear it sung; and let them see how kids responded. Of course, this meant running the risk of confrontation with our detractors, but I felt the possibilities were worth the risk.

About that time I received a phone call from a guy named Ray DeVries. He said he was program coordinator for an organization called The Greater Los Angeles Sunday School Convention (or GLASS.) Ray invited me to do a workshop at the upcoming convention. He said there would probably be about one hundred ministers of music in attendance, and I'd have a chance to show them some of our new music. I readily agreed.

On the day of the workshop, our little room was jam-packed with people; they were standing at the back and sitting on the floor in the aisles. I was nervous but elated. And the workshop went well. When it was over, I made a lunch date with Ray for the following week.

I met Ray at Charley Brown's in Woodland Hills on the appointed day and began to ask him questions about himself. He was an ordained minister with the Reformed Church in America. He was a devoted family man, and he and his wife, Kay, were raising three beautiful kids. Ray also loved music and had a certain vitality for life and all its opportunities that seemed to set him apart.

At one point in our conversation I said, "Ray, why don't you come to work for me. We could do music workshops all over the United States. We'd make a great team—you set 'em up and I'll run 'em." And that's how it started. In due time, Ray did come to work for me, and he began setting up workshops in every city or town that would have us.

The general plan was that he'd start by getting a local Christian bookstore to sponsor us. Then he'd find a choir director in that area to do an evening presentation of our music. Usually, in the beginning, it would be *Tell It Like It Is.* Then he'd find a place to hold the workshop during the day—preferably a neutral spot like a Holiday Inn or a school rehearsal hall, but sometimes a church auditorium. Then, through the combined efforts of Ray and the bookstore manager, promotion would get underway to gather as many choir directors as possible from within a fifty- or one-hundred-mile radius.

The coming months and years would find us crisscrossing the country in all kinds of weather and with varying degrees of success and failure. I remember once in the dead of winter we flew two thousand miles from Los Angeles to a little hamlet in the northeast to hold a workshop for six people, only two of which were bona fide choir directors. Neither the music packets nor the back-up stock for the bookstore arrived in time; the only music we had was what I carried in my briefcase. So we gathered around the piano and looked over each other's shoulders, but the workshop went on even while the snow swirled outside.

On other occasions, our workshops would be attended by two or three hundred people, and over half of them would be ministers of music. The rest would be accompanists, soloists, or just people with a keen interest in music. But almost always we would have a contingent of conscientious objectors to contend with. Occasionally I would get advance warning that trouble was brewing, and I would literally get sick to my stomach. I'd think to myself, "Why am I doing this?" and "Dear God, why do I have to do this?" But I had to do it, so I did it . . . with God's help. The workshop schedule continued to expand, and we did as many as fifty a year.

149

fifteen

FRUITFUL YEARS

The home that Mar and I had bought in Woodland Hills included a connecting garage that had been converted into a couple of odd-shaped rooms with linoleum flooring plus a large hallway with a floor of bare cement. Mar had the linoleum ripped up and a nice, thick, wall-to-wall carpet laid in both rooms and the hallway. Adding some desks and a file cabinet turned the hallway into a third room.

Mar also hired a carpenter to build cupboards along one wall and a ceiling-to-floor bookshelf for records and music on another. Finally, she had the whole outside wall knocked out of the back room and installed sliding glass doors that looked out over the San Fernando Valley. Even though the room was only about ten feet square, it seemed as big as all outdoors with the view through the glass doors.

This became my workroom. There I spent the next thirteen years (when I wasn't doing workshops) putting notes on the page. The other two rooms were occupied by my first two employees, who have remained with me to this very day: my secretary, Lillian Merrill, and my editor, Carl Seal. Through the years their titles have changed commensurate with their salaries, but they themselves remain unchanged in their loyalty and dedication. Another stalwart who joined our staff was Bill Cole. The same Bill Cole who was the foremost studio tenor in the secular field soon turned into the foremost producer of records in the gospel field.

There were many contributors in those beginning years—people who went through the growing pains of a little upstart of a company with an uncertain future. For example, there was Jack Coleman, who wrote the first major work that we actually recorded and published, *City of a King.* I remember the day Jack brought it to me and we went through it together in my living room. I didn't know how we were going to scrape together the money to record it, but we did—and with a full orchestra, plus choir and soloists. For Lexicon/Light to come out with a more-or-less classical cantata such as *City of the King,* which was really quite traditional, sort of confused our protagonists and dumbfounded our antagonists. It was as though we were saying, "Look, we can make music for everybody."

I can recall the first Christian Booksellers Association (CBA) convention that I attended as president of Lexicon/Light. That was 1968. The convention was held in St. Louis, Missouri, and we only had two or three products to display at the Word, Inc., booth.

It was the custom to hold a sales conference adjacent to the CBA convention, and all the Word sales representatives would come together from all over the country to preview the new product that would soon be offered to the public. Word's national sales manager, Bill Jelly, had promised (somewhat begrudgingly, it seemed to me) that I could have ten minutes during the meeting to show our two new books and one new record.

When I arrived in St. Louis, I thought we had some pretty good stuff. But the closer the time came for me to get up in front of those dozen or so reps, the less sure I became. That first time was really rough. I wanted so badly for those guys to like what we were producing that I practically begged them to sell it. My good friend, Cy Jackson, was one of the reps, and I kept glancing his way for reassurance because I knew he was for us.

In retrospect, I guess they were all pulling for us that day, because they surely went out and sold the product. It was because of their efforts that the money kept rolling in, and that meant we could continue to try new things. We could sign new artists and new composers. Without regard for chronological continuity, I'd like to tell about some of the "new things" we tried.

I've already mentioned our first folk musical, *Tell It Like It Is,* but there is one other little story about it that comes to mind. Our first printing was two thousand copies, and when that sold out we reordered, sold out, and reordered again. We were warehousing our music books at the warehouse of the Rodeheaver Company, which Word had purchased, in Winona Lake, Indiana. Bruce Howe, whom I had met during my YFC days, was running that operation and was in charge of all Lexicon product shipped to and from the Winona Lake warehouse.

151

One afternoon I got a call from Jarrell McCracken in Waco, and in an exasperated tone of voice he said, "Ralph, what on earth have you done now?"

I said, "What do you mean?"

He answered, "I just got a call from Bruce Howe, and he's being buried in *Tell It Like It Is* books."

I said, "Oh, that." I went on to explain that since we kept running out of books when we ordered two thousand at a time, I had decided to save five cents a book and all the trouble of reordering by printing one hundred thousand copies all at once.

Jarrell said, "Well, Bruce is fit to be tied. He's running out of room in the warehouse, and he's got books stacked up in his garage and even on his pool table!" Fortunately, we sold them all. In fact, before it was over, we sold well over a quarter of a million copies of *Tell It Like It Is*.

One day Kurt and I received a letter from a man in Princeton, West Virginia, that warmed our hearts and confirmed our belief in what God could do through a simple youth musical. It also pretty well summed up what was happening in churches all across the nation:

Dear Mr. Carmichael and Mr. Kaiser:

Princeton, West Virginia, is not a large town. Its First Baptist Church is not a large church. But this spring the youth of First Baptist gave the people of Princeton something they (nor we) shall ever forget. You had a big part in it, so I knew you would like to know.

We got the *Tell It Like It Is* fever just before Christmas last year. Our Youth Choir of about twenty-five zoomed to fifty before February 1. By April 1 our ideas had outgrown the church building, so we moved to the high school auditorium and three rehearsals a week. The adults of our Youth Committee developed a full portable lighting system, designed and made costumes, designed and built backdrops, and developed and promoted a sixteeen-performance schedule for the month of May.

Somewhere between the middle of April and the first of May, *Tell It* ceased to be just a musical. The singers no longer looked like uncoordinated teenagers. The band was suddenly tuneful, in rhythm, and great! Solo talent, shaky and unsure in January, had blossomed in abundant measure. All of these fruits of arduous rehearsal were gratifying, but what set *Tell It* apart was the growing sense of mission felt by every one of us.

We sought and obtained permission from the Board of Education to present *Tell It* at Princeton High School and Princeton Junior High during school hours. Despite being captive, the kids in these packed auditoriums were wildly enthusiastic.

If we had any doubts before of having a winner, those two performances removed them. On the evening following our matinee at the high school, we made history by having to turn people away from that same auditorium!

We performed at Concord College, Bluefield College, and in the high schools and junior high schools of surrounding communities. Adults and performers alike willingly rearranged their whole lives for the month of May to be faithful to our mission.

The payoff for me—and, I expect, for you—came on a Sunday morning, May 24. The young people had made sure that every one of the group was present for the morning service. A senior girl extended the invitation for accepting Christ or for recommitment to the congregation in general. There was an immediate response. A quartet hummed "Pass It On" while she continued the invitation. She spoke now directly to the group, asking for those to come forward who had felt a deeper commitment to Christ and who wanted to rededicate their lives to His service.

The Holy Spirit descended at that moment as surely as at Pentecost, while in the hush of a moment to be remembered forever, fifty young people came, one by one, to answer the invitation.

Ours is not a demonstrative congregation. Revivals for many years have brought little outward response. But this was revival in the truest sense of the word, and a most moving experience. I would be remiss not to share it with you. Your words on the inside cover of the music book: "The hours of work contained in these pages will only be significant if we hit our intended target . . . to plain-talk kids into a confrontation experience with the truth about God's love and a relationship with His Son.". . . you were on target, dead center. . . .

That, in a sketchy way, is what you have meant to us in these sleepy hills this spring. We wanted you to know how grateful we are to both of you for the many hours you invested. We have never had more fun. We have never felt a deeper love for each other and for our Savior. And we have never been more ready to tackle our next asignment.

We are, however, deeply aware of the tremendous responsibility placed upon us by *Tell It*'s phenomenal success. In this, I earnestly seek your counsel. We can bring together probably sixty-five teenagers, most of them now seasoned and eager, for work on a worthy sequel. What shall it be?

> Sincerely,
> J. B. Copenhaver
> Director of Music

One day in the late 60s, my old friend, Tim Spencer, called me and said he had met a young black guy by the name of Andrae Crouch, who was writing some wonderful songs. Would I be interested in meeting him? I told him I would, and in the course of time I found myself sitting in Tim's office down in Hollywood waiting for Andrae to arrive. He was late, as he has been to every meeting we've had in the last seventeen years. But he finally showed up, as he always does, with a warm and affable greeting that made everyone happy to be there. He thanked me for taking time to hear his songs, and Tim guided him to an old upright piano sitting against the east wall.

Andrae sat down, played an introduction, and started to sing. Then I knew why Tim had asked me to come to his office to hear this guy. Andrae was something special. He was far more comfortable singing and playing than he was walking and talking, and probably enjoyed it more than eating and sleeping.

After a couple of songs, Tim initiated some conversation. Andrae was not a talkative man, but he did express his gratitude for his godly parents and his Christian heritage and also said that his heart went out to the young people who were disillusioned with life and wasted on drugs. He shared his desire to witness to them through music and told how he had put together a singing group called The Disciples, some of whom were ex-addicts he had led to Christ.

I left Tim's office impressed with Andrae but feeling that there was little that I could do for him. On the way home I reviewed what I had heard and seen. Here was a young black man that nobody had heard of. He had a back-up group, some of whom were ex-junkies. His music was a potpourri of rock, jazz, blues, and traditional black gospel. The lyrics were often street-talk (or street vernacular), but they were absolutely scriptural, and they surely moved me.

When I got home, I put the happenings of the afternoon out of my mind because there were many pressing matters at hand. But in the next few days I kept running across the name *Andrae Crouch*—a studio musician asked me if I had heard of Andrae Crouch; one of my copyists said a friend of his had heard Andrae Crouch sing and play.

In 1968 we released the first Andrae Crouch album on the Light Records label. It was the first black gospel record, to my knowledge, ever released by a white gospel label, and it certainly was the first recording by a black artist to be distributed by Word, Inc. How well I remember standing in front of the reps at the 1968 sales conference playing sample cuts from a test pressing called, "Gonna Keep On Singing." Most of the guys personally liked it, but could they sell it? Well, they did, and the rest is history.

In 1971 I was invited to speak before the general assembly of the National Religious Broadcasters (NRB). My topic was "New Trends in Gospel Music." I packed my only suit and tie and flew to Washington, D.C.

As I've said before, public speaking is not my favorite thing, so I developed a good case of nerves before the plane left the ground in Los Angeles. And my nervousness was not helped by the fact that my speech just would not seem to come together. On the plane I hauled out my yellow legal pad and pencil and wrote the title in bold print, but five hours later, all I had to show for my efforts were some doodles and a couple of eight-bar melodies. I checked into the hotel for a couple of hours of sleep, then spent the rest of the morning with that pencil and pad. Still nothing came that was worthy of the momentous occasion. When the time came to suit up, I rationalized that I was too nervous to read from a prepared text anyway, so I'd just wing it.

The assembly hall was quite unique, as I recall; it reminded me of an old English courtroom. There was a speaker's platform with a podium and microphone. The seats for the audience rose from floor level upwards in semicircular tiers. The room seemed comfortably full, with probably five or six hundred distinguished-looking men, mostly in dark suits and ties. I panned back and forth looking for a friendly face, but found nary a one.

With me on the speaker's platform was my old friend from Inglewood, William J. Roberts, who was chairing the meeting and through whom I had received the invitation to speak. Also with us was an old acquaintance and a fine singing preacher (good combination), Wilbur Nelson.

After a few brief preliminaries, I was introduced. My hour had come. I don't really remember what I said; I just rambled. Perhaps my speech might best be described as a slice of my life story, starting with how I played the violin in Dad's church and continuing on to my belief that we ought to experiment with all kinds of music.

When my time was up, I just quit. But before I could get back to my seat, there was some sort of commotion about halfway up the rows of tiers and over to the right. It was some guy yelling—no, it was some guy preaching, preaching loudly with a sort of vibrato and a well-modulated voice. Then, after the first shock, I began to make out what he was saying. He was talking about rock music, the devil, and me—not necessarily in that order, but I got the drift that he disapproved something awful.

Before this man could wind down, a young guy jumped up over to the left and challenged the preacher's remarks by saying that he was in the Christian ministry today because of contemporary music, and he proceeded to put in a good word in my behalf. But before he was through, somebody else was shouting at him for daring to speak out to one of his elders.

Well, before long others had joined in, and the meeting turned into a first-class ruckus, with Rev. Roberts, who was chairing the meeting, pounding the gavel on the lectern trying to restore order. It was a frightening thing to watch.

The man who had spoken against me turned out to be a Dr. Willard Cantelon, who left the hall immediately. The young fellow who had stood up for me was Scott Ross. As I sat there stunned, perspiration burned my eyes and ran down the back of my neck. I sincerely wished I could be someplace else.

The next item on the agenda was to be some inspirational music by Dr. Wilbur Nelson. When he was introduced, he did a very gracious thing. He said that he would like to give up his portion of the program so that I could come back and answer questions from the audience. So I did. But I truthfully cannot remember any of the questions, let alone the answers. I do remember seeking the safety of my hotel room where, in an immature fit of pique, I sent the following telegram to Rev. Cantelon:

Dear Mr. Quixote:
Good luck on your windmill. Letter follows.
Ralph Carmichael

And we did exchange letters:

Dear Rev. Cantelon:
My telegram no doubt raised the temperature of your righteous indignation. It was only meant to test your sense of humor. I value your research, attested to by your remarks, and I have complete confidence in your sincerity. Further, I would defend (to the last man standing) your right to disagree with my position. We do agree, believe it or not, on this: Rock music is a dumb and dull form. But in the name of reason and common sense, let's not waste lances and arrows, precious time and energy, on a sideline argument that will keep us from the main field of battle.

We're really on the same side. The cross is my sign, the resurrection of Christ my hope; the Holy Spirit is that mystical and unfathomable agent that completes the reconciliation process, bringing me back to God my Father, who allowed His Son's blood to be spilled for me, for us. . . . That's what we want kids to know.

You are so gifted, even eloquent. Please don't waste it on a dumb form of music, much less on me. I had these same feelings regarding censorship twenty or twenty-five years ago when a professor of mine at SCBC warned against the evils of showmanship in evangelism as practiced over at Angelus Temple, with their stage productions, worldly music, and cartoonist (that was you, I'm afraid).

Finally, I would not waste a letter to win your approval or to get you to change your mind. I don't want you to change. But we are brothers; let's not fight each other, OK?

Sincerely,
Ralph Carmichael,
President, Lexicon Music, Inc.

P.S.: If you'll invite me to lunch, I'll buy.

Dear Ralph:

Greetings from Washington. I appreciate your taking time to write concerning our meeting at the NRB some days ago. My record library is one of my most cherished possessions. Although it has undergone many changes through the years, your records still remain at the top.

Although our paths have scarcely crossed through the years, this is not true of myself and Brother Roberts. Repeatedly, we have met both at home and overseas. Those who have sat in our audiences will know that there is no man that I have magnified more, both privately and publicly, than Bill Roberts.

I take time to say this not in the way of flattery, but with very honest comment. My love and esteem for each of you as great men in your fields makes it all the more unreasonable that I should have interrupted so rudely the music seminar at the NRB. I am sure Bill could tell you that I am not noted for being quite so rude or unethical.

In covering some of the rock festivals like Woodstock, I know our hearts are mutually disturbed over this destruction of all that is dear to our hearts as Christians and lovers of the genuinely beautiful.

It is this element that arouses my anger and indignation. . . . This is why I impulsively declared there was a side of rock music which should be clarified.

There is as much difference between the type of music I mention and what you have written under the inspiration of God as there is between Satan and God himself.

I appreciate your allowing me to give this explanation. I trust you may have opportunity to pass these comments on, if convenient, to Bill Roberts, my dear friend whom I respect so highly.

Our prayers and love are with you in these amazing days.

Yours sincerely,
Willard Cantelon

P.S.: I'd be delighted to spend an hour together anytime we are on the West Coast, and you let me buy the lunch.

But Dr. Cantelon and I did more than exchange letters. Through the years we have become good friends. We have shared the same platform, and in 1978 Willard brought his son, Paul, to Light Records; we recorded an excellent piano album of his.

In 1984, I was on a panel at NRB, and the topic was "contemporary music," so I asked Dr. Cantelon for a statement. I thought it was beautiful:

> After forty years in international evangelism, I would like to say that the ministry of music and song often opens doors for the presentation of the gospel that no other media could accomplish. As one from the older generation, I am excited today at the presentation of music in modern parables.

I returned from that 1971 NRB convention with a new realization of the great gulf that existed between the musical sound of the church and the secular sound outside the church. I had considered all Christian broadcasters as my allies in my crusade to make church music more relevant. How wrong I was! After some serious pondering over my disappointment, I realized it was a matter of educating the station owners and managers to a new way of thinking. Perhaps I could get them to experiment with me . . . but how?

Finally, I got an idea. It was an expensive one, and it would be a slow process, but it was worth a try. We created what we called the Light Radio Division. I hired a young fellow named Mike Trout, who was a disc jockey at a local Christian radio station. His job was to produce for me a thirty-minute program called *Check The Record*. It was really just a thirty-minute commercial, during which I would interview a Light recording artist and play cuts from his or her latest album. We offered the program free on a weekly basis to any station that would play it.

We had slow going at first, but the program gradually caught on. Eventually we were mailing to several hundred stations, with many of them airing each program more than once a week. (At the height of the show's popularity, we were getting a thousand plays weekly.) Soon we added another format. This was a two-hour disk-jockey show with yours truly playing about thirty-two selections on each show and blank spots every fifteen minutes for commercials that could be sold by each station to local sponsors. For a while we were really in the radio business.

After about five years, I was invited back to NRB to present the music for the opening night concert. Lexicon/Light had just released a new contemporary musical by Jimmy and Carol Owens called, *If My People*. I proposed that we present this in its entirety as the opening-night concert.

With my good friend, Ray DeVries, functioning as mediator and negotiator, we finally got approval, and plans went forward. Thurlow Spurr (of The Spurrlows fame) shipped in a magnificent mass choir from the state of Michigan, complete with a soloist and a "cookin'" rhythm section, and I got my friend, Dr. Richard Halverson, pastor of the great Third Presbyterian Church of Washington, D.C. (and later Chaplain of the U.S. Senate) to be the narrator.

So, with fear and trembling, and complete with a sound system and lighting crew, we presented *If My People* to the 1975 NRB Convention. What a thrill it was to see that audience respond! Before it was over, they were on their feet clapping and singing along.

Later that night, on the elevator, a man wearing a NRB badge leaned close to me and said how much he enjoyed the musical evening and how glad he was that we had changed our music in the past few years to a more acceptable style. I knew then that our patience and efforts were beginning to pay off.

Slowly, from all quarters, Christian leadership and laity alike were participating in the gospel music revolution. Youth choirs were springing up in churches that had never before had youth choirs. Even adult choirs were singing adaptations of the new music, and requests were coming in the mail daily for permission to reprint the lyrics of many of the new songs in church bulletins so that entire congregations could join in and sing them. New artists and new groups were releasing records at an amazing rate. Radio stations and TV producers were beginning to broadcast the new music, and Christian bookstores were beginning to move their record and music departments into more prominent locations.

In April 1974, I received a letter from Dr. Billy Graham that said, in part:

A communication medium is chosen on how well it reaches an audience. In sharing Christ and the gospel, it is natural that the contemporary sound, with its freshness and spontaneity, has become a popular medium, reaching beyond the influence of traditional methods. Christian composers have proven that you can be musically relevant to contemporary society and yet have gospel content which the Holy Spirit can employ.

And to show the growing awareness of the value of the new music on the part of church leadership, let me share a quote from my friend, Dr. Lloyd Ogilvie, pastor of the First Presbyterian Church of Hollywood:

> I believe that we need to run with our Lord on a two-legged gospel. Musically, this means that we must have one foot in the great tradition of creative church music and the other foot squarely planted in the best of the contemporary expressions which touch all dimensions of human experience. The truly great church is one that can blend these together and not fall into the devastating tyranny of the either-or. When we can have the best of Bach, Beethoven, and Mendelssohn and couple it with the viable contemporary expression, then the richness of the total music program enables the growth of persons. Anytime that a person comes to a service, he should have all dimensions of his existence touched profoundly. He should be stretched intellectually, healed emotionally, liberated volitionally, and strengthened physically. Music which is pleasing to a few esoteric musicologists may not touch the deep needs of people who have come to worship.

The decade of the 1970s was exciting, to say the least. The company was growing by leaps and bounds. What an adventure it was! I had long since gotten off the secular music treadmill—working for many artists and many producers and staying up all night in order to meet deadlines.

But actually, not a whole lot had changed. I was still staying up nights fighting deadlines for the gospel recordings we were doing for Light Records, plus keeping office hours during the day and then on weekends flying out to do the workshops and seminars all over the country. But don't feel sorry for me. It was great. This is what I had prayed for and dreamed of all my life!

sixteen

ON OUR OWN

By 1973 our house was bulging at the seams. Mar and I were raising three kids in the main part of the house while running Lexicon/Light in the back three rooms off the kitchen. My staff had grown until every square inch was taken. Desks were back to back and end to end to form sort of a "Rubik's Cube" decor. After the staff left at five o'clock in the afternoon, the copyists would settle in for the night, so our driveway always looked like a parking lot. Conferences with artists and composers spilled over into the living room, and occasionally someone would take a wrong turn and collide with Mar coming out of the bedroom.

Finally one night Mar said, "I wonder what the neighbors think we're running here, with people coming and going at all hours of the day and night?" It was really time to move!

Our new corporate headquarters were only a couple of miles from the house. We took a thousand square feet on the second floor of a just completed office building on picturesque Ventura Boulevard. Along with the new carpet and new phone system, there were several new staff members, and we continued to grow from there.

We also came out with a new product line, for it was about this time that Lexicon published *The New Church Hymnal.* It was a beautifully bound volume of almost seven hundred pages, and it included not only the finest traditional hymns and gospel songs, but also all the new selections that had become popular over the past decade and were beginning to be sung by church congregations of all denominations. What a celebration we had when we introduced it at the 1976 Christian Booksellers Association convention in Atlantic City!

By 1978 we had to move again. This time we took three thousand square feet in another new office building a few blocks down the street. And we kept on growing. Two years later, in 1980, we needed even more space. So I rented twenty-five hundred square feet on the first floor of the Prudential Building in Westlake. I split the office staff, leaving half in Woodland Hills and moving half to the new location.

Now, if you know anything about the geography of the Southern California coast, you may be thinking that it doesn't make a whole lot of sense to have half an office in the San Fernando Valley and half an office twenty miles up the coast in the Conejo Valley. But this was merely a stopgap measure. With all the kids out of the nest, Mar and I indulged a lifelong fantasy and bought a little ranch in Hidden Valley. By degrees we planned to relocate Lexicon "out our way," where office space was fifty-one cents a square foot, as opposed to as high as two dollars a square foot closer to Hollywood.

Meanwhile, back at Word, things had been happening. In 1974, Jarrell McCracken had sold the company to the American Broadcasting Companies, and although he remained as president of Word, there were those who had some misgivings as to the future of the company under the control of such a corporate giant. In the transaction, of course, the 50 percent of Lexicon now owned by Word had passed to ABC, so in essence I was now in partnership with ABC. While I had always had the highest regard for Jarrell's business acumen, I had wondered if the new relationship would bring any restraints, either financially or philosophically, to the artistic freedom we so fervently exercised at Lexicon. And Jarrell had assured me that if ever the time came that I felt uncomfortable with the ABC relationship, he would personally negotiate a deal for me to acquire the outstanding stock from ABC under the most favorable terms possible.

One day, in the spring of 1980, I received a phone call from Jarrell saying that he was coming to California and would like to spend a few hours with me; he had something of importance he wanted to discuss. I said, "Great, we'll have lunch at the ranch."

The appointed day came, and after our usual greetings, Jarrell and I launched into a discussion of one of our favorite subjects—Arabian horses. (Mar and I had bought our first horse in 1972, and now that we lived on the ranch I was able really to enjoy the fulfillment of a lifelong dream.) But as pleasant and as enthusiastic as this conversation was, we both knew the main course was yet to come. Little did I guess just what it was to be.

You can imagine my surprise when, after a slight lull in our "horse talk," Jarrell said, "How would you like to sell out to ABC?" It was a good offer and was made in good faith. We discussed the pros and cons and even got around to establishing a nice round figure.

I'll say this—the power of persuasion is not one of McCracken's underdeveloped talents. It was tempting to think about the offer in a way. But on the other hand, I just knew I couldn't do it. There were future plans that might never reach fruition and tentative commitments that might never be kept if I gave up control and walked out now.

That night Mar and I discussed the offer at some length, but in the end the decision was an easy one. Not only did I turn the offer down; I made a counteroffer to buy Lexicon/Light from ABC. The only problem was that, when ABC was the prospective buyer, I had argued the value of the company up in price. Now the shoe was on the other foot, and as the seller ABC agreed wholeheartedly about how valuable the company really was. In time, however, the attorneys hammered out the fine print, and in June of 1980 I bought Word's half of the company.

Oh what a celebration we had! Prayers had been answered; dreams were coming true. Now, having sole ownership of the company, I could take it in the direction I felt the good Lord wanted us to go, even though at the time I was not sure just where that would be. Whatever uncertainties accompanied our new "total control" position, there was never a doubt concerning the continued growth of the company, and so we plunged headlong into our expansion plans. We now had our own marketing and distribution staff and had severed all ties with Word and ABC except the ties of friendship.

About ten miles northwest along the freeway from the Westlake office is a sleepy little town of Newbury Park, where great herds of cattle once grazed on the Danielson Ranch. It was there, just a stone's throw from the freeway, that we moved in 1981. Vacating the other two offices, our whole staff was all together at last in approximately twenty thousand square feet of office and warehouse space. In addition, we leased another twenty thousand square feet building back in Warsaw, Indiana, for our fulfillment center; all Lexicon publications and Light albums and cassettes would be shipped from there to points all over the United States.

Naturally, since we had all this space, we started hiring people to fill it. We were really ready for growth now! Instead of saying, "Hi, Mar, I'm home," I generally burst through the door each evening with, "Hey, Mar, you won't believe what happened today!" There were always new artists, new composers, new ideas, and new opportunities.

Unfortunately, there were also new pressures, not the least of which was *cash flow*. I had lived very happily for over half a century and had never heard those words put together before, but they would soon grow to be the bane of my existence.

Because of my long-time interest in horses, I have learned some things about training them. One is that if a horse gets away with a "bad thing" three times in a row, you are likely to end up with a horse that has a bad habit that is very difficult to break. Likewise, if a horse does a "right thing" and is instantly rewarded three times in a row, you have established what could be the start of a successful training program.

With humans, however, it's a little more complicated, for with our superior intellect, we can really louse things up. For example, if we do three "right things" in a row, we might get the idea that we're just made that way and that everything we do will be right. Wouldn't we all like to be infallible?

Well, I'm afraid that's what happened to me. After being rejected and ridiculed through the 1950s and most of the 1960s, the 70s had turned out to be my decade, so to speak, and maybe I was well on my way to thinking that I could do no wrong. Then, all of a sudden, I did a half-dozen dumb things right in a row.

The first was paying cash for ABC's Lexicon stock in two payments just months apart, which practically bankrupted my company.

Next, we signed some artists' contracts that were really too rich for our blood—or rather, for our pocketbook.

Next, to finance our expansion, I went to a new bank and got a large loan without reading the fine print. (More on that later.)

Also, I allowed some internal problems to develop in the company—problems having to do with leadership and management and snafus caused by various departments' being out of phase with each other. (At one time a consultant told us that we were operating at about 30 percent efficiency!)

The last straw was placed on the camel's back without any help from me. In 1981 the economy started down a hill so steep that the rumble of its momentum shook even the impregnable foundations of the gospel music field. How well I remembered interviews I'd given to broadcasters and journalists in which I had declared with conviction, "People may be short on spendable dollars, but they will always find a way to buy gospel music." In fact, one time I had gotten overconfident enough to predict that the tougher the economy got, the more people would turn to gospel music for inspiration and comfort. And I really believed that.

Well, let me tell you, between the internal problems (those peculiar just to our company) and the external problems (those endured industry-wide), we were about to go through an experience that no one should have to endure more than once in a lifetime!

In March of 1982, Don Butler, executive director of the Gospel Music Association, called and asked if I would accept the position of president-elect of the GMA. And he requested an overnight decision. Well, you can guess what Mar and I talked about over dinner that evening. We both knew it was a high honor to be asked to serve. On the other hand, the difficulties we were having cast clouds of apprehension over every new opportunity that came along, including this one.

Finally I said, "I'm gonna do it," and Mar said, "If you feel you should, I'll support you all the way." I was installed as president-elect (under Frances Preston, who was president) at the Dove Awards, 3 March 1982, during GMA Week in Nashville.

The second board meeting of the Gospel Music Association that I attended was held the first week of May 1982 at beautiful Lake Barkley in Kentucky. And it was difficult for me to get on that plane knowing that during my absence the company was losing thousands of dollars each day.

It was really quite a confusing situation. In monthly meetings with the bankers, which I attended in company with my young vice president, the year-to-date financial statements always looked pretty good, and I would come away with my head in a bubble of optimism. But the next day we'd have a "cash requirements" meeting back in my office, and a totally different picture would be presented to me. As a company, we were bleeding to death! For the past four months we had repeatedly discussed plans for cutting our overhead, but the plans were never implemented. We were like an automobile with no low gear, no neutral, and no reverse—just high gear. And we seemed to be hurtling down-hill fast.

To get to Lake Barkley, you fly into Nashville and travel by car into the breathtaking beauty of southern Kentucky. I told myself that these days away from the corporate turmoil would be good for me, and I resolved to lose myself in the secluded change of pace provided by the GMA board session and the mealtime fellowship with the other board members.

But that's not exactly what happened at Lake Barkley. We checked in at the old wooden lodge and found the way to our respective rooms. Upon entering, my eyes went instantly to the phone, and I knew I could find out what was happening back home by just dialing. And dial I did. During the week I left the board meetings on an hourly basis for brief phone calls. I absented myself from the dining room for long phone calls. During the night, while others slept, I sketched out Plan A, Plan B, Plan C—then discarded all three, only to start over.

Before the week was over, I knew what I had to do. I made an appointment with my executive vice president for the following Monday morning at eight o'clock.

I seldom wear a suit and tie to the office, but on Monday, 10 May 1982, I did. What I was about to do was one of the three most difficult tasks of my life, and I prayed that God would help me do it with mercy and dignity. Starting with my executive vice president, I fired twenty-three Lexicon/Light employees that day. During the days ahead I called in twenty lease cars and let go of about ten thousand square feet of warehouse space.

But that wasn't the worst of it. In June of 1982 I discovered a large cache of checks that had been processed but never mailed out. Because we had no funds to cover the checks, they had been allowed to accumulate in a bottom drawer. And this undoubtedly had been going on for several months.

This explained why we looked good at the banker's meetings but not so good at our own "cash requirements" meetings. Because the checks had been processed, those amounts had been taken off the computer printout for accounts payable. Now, when the checks were voided and the amounts reentered in the accounts-payable column, the bankers became more than somewhat concerned.

It was about sundown one June evening, and I had just returned from a horseback ride in the mountains behind our ranch. I had been doing some pretty heavy thinking and praying about what I should do. After putting the horse in his box stall, I walked slowly back up to the house, planning the approach I would use to present my idea to Mar. It turned out to be simple and direct: "Maybe we should sell the company." The thought didn't exactly send a tingle of joy up my spine, but at least it was an honorable way to see that the creditors would be paid off a hundred cents on the dollar. And if I found the right buyer, they might sign me back on as an employee; perhaps I could even remain as president.

I surmised that surely the value of the company would far exceed its indebtedness. I even put some numbers down on paper to assure Mar that we would still be able to live comfortably. My practical little Mar said, "You know, you probably don't have to sell, but it might not be a bad idea to shop around for a good buyer just in case you decide you want to."

Little did we realize how much shopping I would do and how badly I would want to sell before it was over. At first, however, I was hesitant and moved with reluctance. I just couldn't get used to the idea that God had brought us this far, only to ask us to give it all up.

The accountants prepared a financial statement showing all of our assets and liabilities, which any prospective buyer would need to see. And of course the statement looked pretty grim. It showed that the company actually had a negative net worth, even with over two million dollars in accounts receivable and current inventory! In exasperation I argued that they had not taken into consideration the three-and-a-half million dollars' worth of valuable record masters and two-and-a-half million dollars' worth of priceless engraving plates that were in storage—plus over twenty-five hundred copyrights, the numerous artists' contracts, and the label name. The accountants patronizingly explained that you can't show any of those things on a balance sheet.

Well, over the eight-month period from late summer of 1982 to the spring of 1983, I stood with hat in hand eleven times, trying to sell my company to nine different buyers. (With two of the prospects we negotiated twice.) I'll list them in alphabetical order: Al Bruner, Steve Lorenz, Bob McKenzie, MTM (Mary Tyler Moore), Joel Nagy, John Ward, Marty Winkler, Word/ABC, and Pat Zondervan.

During the summer and fall of 1982, I saw acts of courage at the office on the part of my remaining staff members to equal that found in front-line trenches. And Mar was a bastion of stength as well. Each evening she would listen to my recital of the day's activities and would make copious notes, from which we would develop our plan of action for the next day.

We found ways to economize that I had never thought possible. I spent several hours each day talking on the phone with suppliers and vendors or meeting them in person, arranging better credit terms or extended payment schedules. Our company payroll day was delayed first one week and finally two weeks, and the executives were asked to take pay cuts. Lil, my secretary, went on a four-day week. One of my executives volunteered to cut back to a three-day week. Actually, I don't believe either of them worked any less; they just got paid less. And I went off salary for a full year.

In October of 1982, my account representative at the bank (the one who had arranged our company loan) and his assistant asked for an appointment. We had not missed a payment, so I thought it would be just a routine meeting. They told me that they still believed that we could pull out of our tailspin, but that as the end of the year was approaching, it was quite apparent we were going to show a loss. That would put us in violation of our covenant of net worth. I said, "What's a covenant of net worth?" That's when they explained that the fine print of our loan document called for Lexicon to show a profit of two hundred thousand dollars for 1982—a figure we clearly were not going to reach.

My banker and his assistant had an idea they felt was certain to raise the comfort level of their superiors and bank auditors. They proposed that I give the bank a second lien on my ranch. They assured me it was just a formality and would be a simple thing to do. I thanked them and said it sounded OK to me, but "Could I run it by my wife and John Caldwell, my attorney?"

Mar voted "no", and John said, "Absolutely no!" even though I argued that it would only be for a few months, until we got back into a profit position. So I stalled for awhile, until it became certain that not only were we not going to have a two-hundred-thousand-dollar profit in 1982, but we were going to have a monumental loss.

The bank started pressing me, and I gave in. It seemed the sensible thing to do. After all, with just a couple of signatures, the bank would leave our loan in place, and we could proceed with business as usual. So, much to the dismay of Mar and John, I gave the bank a second on our ranch.

One Tuesday in November, I returned from a luncheon appointment to find an IRS agent sitting next to the switchboard. She announced that we were several months delinquent in remitting our payroll taxes. I invited her into my office and called in the company head of finance. It was all very cordial and civilized, and my man explained that cash had been temporarily tight and, since he hadn't received any notices, he had used the delay to our financial advantage. Now, he said, he would be happy to work out a payment schedule. She smiled and said she would get back to us after she had consulted with her superior.

The next day (Wednesday), I received a call from the head of the IRS office of Ventura County. He informed me that the lady agent had been transferred to another office and that I was to be in his office at nine o'clock Friday morning with the six-figure payment in full.

I said, "But what about the pay-out schedule we talked about." He literally yelled his answer, "Be here with a certified check, or I'll shut you down immediately!"

Stunned, I hung up the phone. For the first time that I could remember since my childhood days, I was really afraid. Mar asked, "Who was that?" And I answered, "I have to make another call; I'll tell you later."

How grateful I was to reach John Caldwell so late in the day. I told him my story, and there was a moment's pause. He said, "I'm going to give you the name and phone number of an ex-IRS agent who is now in the business of consulting with people with problems like this one. Tell him I told you to call . . . and then do exactly what he tells you to do!"

I'll call him Jim. He was a kindly old gentleman—soft-spoken and deliberate. He asked me how much we owed, and I told him. He asked me how much I could raise in twenty-four hours. I told him I didn't know. He said to get as much as I could (either a cashier's check or certified check) and to meet him for a briefing at eight-fifteen on Friday morning. From there we would drive to the IRS office.

He showed up Friday morning right on time and quickly gathered the information he needed, asking to scan certain documents, wanting to know how much money I had raised and how much could be paid back on a weekly basis. Then we were on our way with the admonition, "When we get there, let me do the talking." He asked me if I understood the magnitude of our corporate wrong; I said that I did and that it was the first time in eighteen years anything like this had happened. I got the idea that his ability to help me this time was somehow connected to his sincere belief that it would never happen again.

At the meeting, Jim was able to negotiate a way for us to pay off our taxes over a period of time we could live with. We did. And I'll be eternally grateful for his advice and help.

seventeen

A MEASURE OF GRACE

I am by nature stubborn. Mom says I get that from my father. I am also sufficiently mean and ornery enough to be able to take my share of hurt. Still, I want to say that the measure of grit and grace that it was taking to get through these days was beyond me. But it was not beyond God.

Of course, I did have to experiment a little bit as to how to find access to His resources. A lot of Christians may tell you it's as easy as falling off a log, and maybe in theory that's true, but in practice. . . . Well, that's the whole thing; it takes practice, and lots of it. Even falling off a log can get you skinned up if you're not in condition and haven't been doing it on a regular basis!

I didn't mean to stretch this into a sermon about how "His grace is sufficient." What I did want to say was that sometimes God slips us that little extra strength and courage in the form of a friend or two—somebody who has been over the road before and has a strong shoulder to lean on, or someone whose vision is a little clearer than our own on certain matters. The list of champions who came to my aid would fill a chapter. There was Dick Berg, a turnaround specialist for sick companies, who taught me the value of communicating with our creditors; Toby Walker, a member of Lexicon's board, who told me, "When you've had all you can take, decide to take one more day, and pretty soon this year will be behind you"; Peter Horne, a management consultant, who taught me how to read a balance sheet; Mary Crowley, Hy Lesnick, John Ward, and Earl Winburn, who lent me money to keep going. And, of course, I thank my attorneys, John Caldwell and Chuck Hurewitz, for their patience, wisdom, and unerring steadfastness. It begins to read like an acceptance speech at the Grammy Awards, doesn't it? With all of this support, we were bound to win. And yet, for a while, things went from bad to worse.

It seems that rumors of our demise spread like cancer out to our dealers, some two thousand of them across the country, and they became increasingly reticent to pay for product. At one point, over 50 percent of our accounts receivable were more than ninety days delinquent. With no cash, we were unable to keep up production schedules or to pay royalties, and many of our artists and composers became disenchanted. Some asked to be released from their contracts; others waited in silence. We had very little new product to ship, and what little we had suffered for lack of promotion dollars to bring it to the attention of the public.

On 17 December 1982, with Christmas just around the corner, I had to fire another twenty-seven people, and there was no money to give them severence pay. The remaining skeleton crew was furloughed, without pay, until after New Year's.

No words can describe the way this made me feel. The humiliation over the perpetration of this catastrophe and the sorrow for the hurt I had brought to so many families, especially the week before Christmas, nearly crushed the breath right out of me. Every day I rode out into the mountains or down through Sycamore Canyon—anywhere to escape from view and be alone to think.

I was really beginning to identify with Job, whose story I had heard in sermons and Bible classes all my life. Once or twice an acquaintance, trying to be helpful, would hint that the reason for my plight was either lack of faith or the presence of sin in my life. After close examination, I found what appeared to be traces of both, and I vowed to monitor each of the two more closely in an effort to raise the level of the former while lowering the level of the latter.

In the course of one of these introspective sessions, I did come across a possible root of my problems. What if I had lied to myself and everybody about wanting to own all of Lexicon/Light so I could take it where I felt "God wanted it to go"? What if the real reason had been plain and simple—pride of ownership? I began to examine my motives. Maybe it had become too important to me to be president and sole owner of a successful record label and publishing company.

This was not just a fleeting thought; I worked on it every day over a period of weeks and months. And while in the beginning of this time of reversal I found the idea of selling the company almost unbearable, by the end of 1982 I hoped every day and prayed every night for one of the prospective buyers to go through with a deal. But nothing materialized.

One night over dinner I said, "Well, Mar, if we can't sell the company, maybe we'll have to sell the ranch." It didn't seem like a very good idea, and the words sounded ominous, but over the next few days we looked at the possibility this way and that way. And we decided just in case we were faced with a "worst possible case" situation, it might be prudent to list the ranch with a broker. We agreed on a price that would leave ample cash to pay off all our personal and corporate debt, and with heavy hearts both Mar and I signed the listing papers.

Every morning when I left for the office and every sundown when I returned to the ranch, the big, bold, red-and-white "For Sale" sign was a reminder of the tightening noose around my neck. Interest rates had risen to over 20 percent, and the economy was in terrible shape. Despite my rash statements years before that people would always buy gospel music and records no matter what sort of financial crisis the country went through, our sales had plummeted. Even with all the layoffs (from eighty-eight to fourteen employees) and the reduction in office space (from twenty thousand square feet to four thousand square feet), we were just barely able to service our loans with monthly principal and interest payments.

Oh, I was willing to sell, all right: "Just take it. . . . Take it all— the company, the ranch, everything." I told God that since He had given it to me in the first place, He was welcome to have it back. Christmas of 1982 was not much fun.

Shortly after the first of the year (January 1983), our account representative at the bank left the position suddenly. Then, a few weeks later, his assistant also left. While it was unsettling to be without their friendly influence, I relied on the promise that, having given the bank a second lien on the ranch, we were in a secure position, and I knew we were current on our payments. So you can imagine my surprise when I received a phone call from an unfamiliar voice out of the San Francisco branch of the bank announcing that they were going to foreclose— not just on the company, but on the ranch as well.

I said, "Wait a minute, you can't do that!" But they could and they did. That night, when I told Mar, she was stunned in disbelief. Then she got angry, and finally she cried, and I held her tight as the sobs shook her little body. The notice of foreclosure papers was received dated April 6, and the clock started ticking down to a foreclosure auction set for 27 July 1983.

Our lives changed a lot on that day, and they probably won't ever be exactly the same again. We spent hours, days, and weeks considering our options. First, if we could sell the company, if only for the indebtedness, that would lift the second on the ranch. It might also leave me unemployed, or with a very small salary. The second option would be to sell the ranch and pay off the bank.

We now pursued both of these possibilities with new desperation. The word unavoidably got out, however, that the company was in foreclosure, and the last three prospective buyers backed off and took the position of "Let's wait and see what happens."

I don't know how, but word also got out that the ranch was in foreclosure. We have a stout pair of nine-foot wrought-iron security gates at the entrance of the property and a speaker phone with which visitors can announce their arrival. One evening at sundown the gate bell rang, and I asked over the intercom, "Who's there?" Keep in mind that this conversation is carried by loudspeaker over the whole ranch and can be heard for some distance out across the valley by several of our neighbors. In response to my question came an answer loud and clear: "I understand the Carmichael ranch is in foreclosure, and I'd be interested in. . . ."

I interrupted with a vengeance and a curt dismissal: "You must be mistaken." He rang two more times, but we huddled in silence within the protection of our home nestled in the oak grove two hundred yards up the slope from where the intruder waited. When we finally heard the car motor retreat in the distance, we breathed a sigh of relief— for the moment. But the experience drove home the fact that we were actually losing our home. This was really happening, and now the whole world knew about it. From that time on we received letters and phone calls from several other "interested parties," all anxious to "pick up the pieces."

There was a third option—to get a new jumbo loan on the ranch. It would have to be large enough to pay off the original loan as well as the second lien we had taken out to cover the company loan.

There were, of course, a few minor problems with that option. For starters, no one wants to make a large loan on a property that is listed for sale. Mar solved that. She called the broker and said, "Come and take your sign down."

Not as easy to solve was the fact that we were in foreclosure. Do you think you'd have nerve enough to ask a lending institution for a million-and-a-half-dollar loan on a property that was in foreclosure? You would if it was the only thing left to do. Over the next six weeks, Mar contacted every loan broker or lender that showed even the slightest promise. Altogether she assembled twelve loan packages; and we'd deliver them and then hope and pray. About half were flat-out "no." Some turned into an interview, and a couple even called for an appraisal. Dick Berg even contacted some lenders that specialize in equity funding and who charge as high as eight points for loan fees, plus 5 percent over the prime interest rate. They weren't interested.

Meanwhile, the last prospective buyer for the company was due to give me a fourth "final" answer. What had started out to be a reasonable offer was now down to "We might consider taking over the company for whatever the existing debts are."

Even though the listing broker on the ranch complained at not having a sign out front, he still showed the place occasionally. We always had a flurry of action just before the listing would run out and come up for renewal. Among the "lookers" were the likes of Mrs. Sylvester Stallone, Kenny Rogers' uncle, Olivia Newton-John and an eccentric scientist who wanted his mother-in-law to buy the place for him so he could have a pure water spring in the event of a nuclear war. But we still were looking for our first firm offer.

Usually, when you're standing barefoot on a hot spot, there's a place you can step for relief. If you're on burning sand, you can move quickly to the beach towel. If you're on sun-baked pavement, you can scurry to the cool, green lawn. But during that time of my life, it seemed as if I was standing smack-dab in the middle of ten square miles of hot tin roofs, with burning sand and sun-baked pavement all lined up as far as the eye could see, and not a speck of shade in sight.

During all this turmoil, it was business as usual over at Lexicon/Light. Well, not really "as usual." The place was feverish, and our little crew was desperately fighting for survival. All hands were working long hours for short dollars. By the end of the first quarter, the lowering of interest rates promised a possible positive effect on sales of records and music. I hired back my national sales manager, whom I had let go in 1982, and he in turn began to put in place a small sales staff. We didn't have much product to sell—only three new albums in the first half of 1983. They were *Together,* a compilation album we produced for World Vision; an album by Buck and Dottie Rambo called *Son of Thunder, Daughter of Light;* and *Chariots of Fire* by Dino. We needed more momentum.

The next big push, if we had any push left, would be the July releases, which we needed to display at the CBA convention to be held in mid-July. From the record division, under Bill Cole, we would need at least four good new album releases. From the print division, under

Carl Seal, we would need at least three new choral books, plus a half-dozen octavos (single choir pieces). The question was, in our present plight, would the artists still record for us? Would our composers still compose for us? And if so, could we pay the costs of production, manufacturing, and marketing?

Thinking about the way we were making short-term decisions gave me a strange feeling. Not that it was necessarily wrong—I just didn't feel comfortable. I'd ask myself, "Is releasing new records and books in order to pay off old debts a valid reason for releasing new records and books?"

I decided, "No, it isn't . . . if that is the only motivation or even the prime motivation." I made the decision that I would not let my present plight tarnish the sincerity of my youthful commitment. I had dedicated myself to God and had brought Him my dreams, desires, and deepest longings, and that relationship was still alive. My deal was still good, and the partnership between me and God was still working. I had artists and composers I believed in. Their work needed to be heard by the church and by the world as well.

It seemed plain as day that we needed to get back to basics—and I included myself in the "we." If we challenged our artists and composers to a new level of effective creativity, and if our staff responded in kind, then we would once again be a red-hot team, working together to bring the Good News of the gospel to the world through our music. Then, if we added a heaping measure of good stewardship, a lot more right decisions, and very few mistakes, before long those bad debts would melt away. Instead of the profit and loss controlling us, we would march to the beat of a loftier motivation, and all else would fall into step.

It sounded good, but of course it wasn't easy . . .good things seldom are. Nevertheless, we went to work with new confidence.

In the spring of 1983, I was installed as president of Gospel Music Association (GMA), and was never so proud of anything in my life. But I returned from that great celebration in Nashville called GMA Week (the one that ends with the annual Dove Awards) with the gnawing fear that I could possibly be the first president in the history of the organization to disgrace the office by losing his home, his business, and his TRW rating (computerized credit status) in one fell swoop—and all that before I had a chance to preside over my first board meeting.

I decided to cut my losses by resigning, so I called Don Butler, the executive director, and told him that in the light of recent and coming events I felt I should step down. When I finished speaking my piece, there was just a moment's pause, during which I thought I heard the intake of a big breath. Then, with that booming basso profundo, he roared, "You'll do no such thing." So I didn't.

Every now and then during this period, a well-meaning colleague, friend, or acquaintance would ask me, "Have you written any new albums lately?" or "When are you going to write another musical?" They just didn't realize how exciting my life was at the moment. Besides, a guy has to save some time to lie awake nights and worry . . . and pray. (It's funny how we insist on trying to combine the two.)

When a prospective buyer cannot be reached for a final answer on whether or not you have a deal, then you probably don't have a deal. But one gets dumb when one gets desperate. Day after day and phone call after phone call, I chased after rainbows, until I was finally administered the coup de grâce. There was no deal. They were not going to buy my company. That was buyer number nine and deal number eleven. We were in foreclosure. There were no other prospects. And time was running out.

Meanwhile, back at the ranch. . . . Not a single property had sold in Hidden Valley for two years, and it was not likely that someone would rush in to buy our ranch. So that left only the possibility of getting a loan, which at the time also seemed like an impossibility. Wouldn't you feel safe in catagorizing such a likelihood an impossibility after being turned down twelve times?

The wife of our realtor called one afternoon. She said she knew a loan broker who might be able to help us. "Wonderful," we said, "what shall we do?" Mar put together another loan package, and the next afternoon, as instructed, we delivered it to a small, sedate, but very elegant home in Beverly Hills.

A young man with a British accent answered the door and took the package. "Yes," he was expecting me, and "Yes," he was the loan broker, and "Yes," he would be in touch with me. A week later, Mar and I sat across a desk from him and listened to him explain that he had found an exceptional loan possibility with a small Savings & Loan company whose head office was in a sleepy little hamlet just south of Pasadena called Alhambra. He said that when the deal was set he would let us know.

There were days of waiting. Then they called for an appraisal. Then there was more waiting. And then we learned what the terms would be. They were not to be believed. At that time, nobody was getting nor giving that kind of loan. And, of course, we didn't actually have it yet. But we prayed and hoped.

In terms of preparation for CBA, the days sped by. There was so much work to do: recording sessions, mix-downs, mastering, and photo sessions for album covers. One day Bill Cole brought a message from Sandra Crouch, a truly gifted soloist and composer in her own right. She knew all about our problems. She knew we had not been able to keep current with the royalty payments due her brother, Andrae. She knew we didn't have any money to spend. But she said she wanted to do an album for Light Records. She believed in us, and she had written a number of brand-new songs. So what were we waiting for? She got her own band together and recorded with the choir from her father's church. Her album and choral book, entitled, *We Sing Praises,* were scheduled for release in mid-July at CBA. Dear Sandra, I'll always be grateful.

In June we got the loan commitment. The terms, by the way, were one-and-a-half million dollars for thirty years, fully amortized at twelve percent interest. Escrow opened in forty-eight hours and was to fund in about thirty days. Hallelujah, it was time to celebrate! But wiser heads than ours warned us not to. We were cautioned to look at the whole situation logically; if it was too good to be true, it probably was not true. And I knew they were right. We put the celebration on hold and kept working and praying.

Bill Cole did it! We were going to go to the CBA convention in Washington, D.C., with our full quota of product. The albums were: Thurlow Spurr's Festival of Praise album, *Jesus;* Tramaine Hawkins' album, *Determined;* the great Winans' album entitled *Long Time Comin';* and our surprise album, Sandra Crouch's *We Sing Praises.*

And Carl Seal did it too. He gave us three great new choral books: *I Feel Like Singing,* by Walter Hawkins; *Jesus,* (Festival of Praise, Volume 4), by Thurlow Spurr; and *We Sing Praises,* by Sandra Crouch, plus six new octavos and a brand-new set of solo tracks, Series #5, comprised of twelve selections for high and low voice.

Mar and I were like a couple of kids when we boarded the plane from California to Washington, D.C. The convention was fabulous. Our sales staff, consisting of five field representatives under the direction of Neil Hesson, had arrived ahead of schedule to set up the booth, and it looked beautiful. Spirits were high, and expectancy filled the air.

The only problem, of course, was the pesky uncertainty as to whether or not our loan would fund in time to beat the bank foreclosure. Mar and I did our best to conceal our anxiety as we made appearances in the booth and kept our daily schedule of appointments.

We stayed in daily contact with my secretary, Lillian, as well as John Caldwell, my attorney: "Has the broker called? Has the loan officer called?"

"No news is good news," Lillian reminded us. "Hope for the best and plan for the worst" was Mr. Caldwell's admonition.

The CBA convention closed on Thursday, and that night Mar and I hosted a dinner at a Chinese restaurant for the staff. During dinner, many questions were asked about the future of the company. These guys had wives and kids, and they were grasping for any scrap of information that would raise their security level.

I understood that. We were all in the same boat. My answers were made up in equal portions of what I hoped and what I believed. It had been a great week, and they had done a fantastic job of regaining credibility with the hundreds of dealers who came by the booth. They not only had sold product; they had sold a new sense of confidence in the company. And as I looked into their faces that night, even I felt a new confidence. With a team like that, we could win.

There is always a Gospel Music Association board meeting scheduled immediately following the CBA convention. As president, I moved through the three days of sessions in a zombielike trance. I hoped nobody noticed, but my tolerance threshhold for suspense was dangerously close to being reached.

The board meeting concluded Saturday night. Mar was all packed, and Sunday morning we headed for Dulles Airport. Usually Mar and I never run out of things to talk about. But suddenly we just fell silent. It wasn't that we were shutting each other out, because there actually was great comfort in the awareness of each other's presence. I guess we both knew that our job now was to wait in patience. Wait and trust. Wait and see. Wait until July 27.

We waited during the cab ride to the airport, and we waited throughout the long flight home. On the morning of July 27, our patience was rewarded. The record will show that on the very day that marked the end of the foreclosure period, at which time both the Carmichael Ranch and Lexicon Music, Inc. were to be placed up for auction, funds in the amount of one-and-a-half million dollars were released to us through escrow.

Mar and I rose early, had our usual breakfast, dressed as if it were Sunday, and headed for Alhambra. It was a warm, bright, clear day . . . well, let's face it; it was just about the prettiest day we had ever seen. When it was over, the bank was paid off, and we had a new lease on life.

There was another very practical benefit. Because of the favorable terms, the new loan actually cost eight thousand dollars per month less to service than had the two previous loans. In other words, our cash-flow problem suddenly improved to the tune of eight grand a month!

The Lord giveth and the Lord taketh away. But when He giveth it all back again, what does that mean? I'm not really sure. But I do know that it changes the way you perceive the value of things. I mean all things—material and spiritual, earthly and eternal.

It's not that material things necessarily have less value than they had before. Perhaps they just have a different value. And in one sense, they may even have a "better" value, in that I came to realize they are not mine in terms of "sole proprietorship," but have been assigned to me in trust. I must neither dote on material things nor squander them. I must guard them gratefully and treat them prudently, for I want to be a profitable servant.

Getting well takes time. We had been granted the time, now I wanted to use it wisely and focus all my energies on recovery. Back in 1982, my consulant friend Dick Berg had told me one day over a tuna-fish sandwich, "If you ever pull through this mess, I know a young fellow you should hire as your executive vice president." And he had said some pretty glowing things: "I wouldn't start a business without him," and "If he called right this minute and asked me for fifty grand, I'd get it to him this afternoon, and then tomorrow I'd ask what he wanted it for."

Call it presumption, call it faith—I had the audacity to look him up in early 1983 when I couldn't even pay the salaries of the employees I had and hadn't taken a paycheck myself for over a year. He already had a great job running the publishing division of a large, nationally known Christian organization called Gospel Light. His name was David Malme.

I made a luncheon appointment with David up in the little town of Ventura for our first meeting. I was impressed. He didn't know anything about music, and I didn't know much about business, so I figured we'd make a great team. For our second meeting I took Bill Cole along. He was impressed.

Over the next six months, there were many meetings and phone calls and long hours of poring over financial statements, and digging for information and more information. After he and his wife, Jan, had given the decision a lot of prayerful consideration, David met me early one morning at Jack's Deli in Westlake and opened with a statement that had the ring of sweet lyrics. He said, "I think this company can be turned around!" In October of 1983, David Malme joined our staff as executive vice president.

We ended 1983 with only a small profit, but the good part was that we were releasing fine new albums and publishing exciting new music. And each month, after the current bills were paid, the rest went to retire the back debt. We had a long way to go, but we were moving forward.

finale

Today, Lexicon/Light still continues to grow, slowly but steadily, signing a new artist here and re-signing an old artist there, and adding new employees cautiously as our sales increase. I cannot believe the quality of people who continue to join our staff.

The state of our accounts receivable have improved remarkably. In 1982, half of our accounts were ninety days overdue. Now only 5 percent are past ninety days, and some months the number drops as low as 2 percent. Sales for 1984 showed a 46 percent increase over 1983.

With the company doing well again, Mar and I have had more time to enjoy the ranch, and I am writing music again. Some of the kids are married and giving us grandkids, and God is still in control. (He always was, of course, but a time or two there I had begun to wonder if He hadn't dozed off.)

We're having company Christmas parties again, and last Christmas I grew misty-eyed to see all the guys in suits and ties, the gals in festive dresses, everyone smelling of perfume and cologne. As Mar and I shook their hands and looked into loving faces, a sort of silent message was exchanged: We're still here, and we're going to make it. And God is with us!

In closing, I'd like to say that I was going to write this book whether it had a happy ending or not. As a matter of fact, there was a time when it wouldn't have ended very happily. It was half written by 1983, and my good publisher sort of wanted it out by July of that year, in which case the ending might have really been a "downer."

But my story would have been essentially the same whether or not

God had given me back my company and my ranch. I feel that He has given me a job to do—to communicate gospel truth through music. And I have done that job while living in a dingy motel room and begging someone else to record and publish my music the same as I have while being president of my own corporation.

I hope I don't have to endure circumstances like those hard years again, but if I have to, I can. Who knows, I'm very healthy and may live long enough to go broke again! In that case, I'll write another book and tell about it!

But whatever happens, I won't change my tune to "He's *Almost* Everything to Me." A deal's a deal. And I will always love and praise him with my music.

coda

MUSIC AS A MINISTRY VEHICLE*

My subject today is "Music As a Ministry Vehicle." But first, let's think a little bit about just exactly what music really is and where it came from.

MUSIC IS AN ART

From a letter I received from Dr. Billy Graham dated 4 April 1974, I share with you the following: "Besides poetry, music is the only art that seems to have been cultivated to any extent in ancient Israel."

Yes, music is art, and the creation of this art form is described in glorious detail over and over again throughout the Old Testament. And it was all done at the command of God through his prophets.

There was that great and glorious concert performed by Hebrew singers and musicians to celebrate their rescue from Pharaoh's army. There they were, hundreds of thousands of people gathered on the far side of the Red Sea, rehearsing a great antiphonal chorale—a work of art. Exodus 15:1–18 has the male choir singing the stanzas and Exodus 15:20–21 has all of the women, led by Aaron's sister, Miriam, singing the chorus and playing their timbrels (hopefully on beats two and four.)

Centuries later, there was also music in the Temple. In 1 Chronicles

---

* Publisher's note: The following is the text of a speech given by Ralph Carmichael at a dinner at the Word Publishing Sales Conference, December 1985. It is included here because we feel it gives a fitting perspective on the music that has been the theme of Ralph Carmichael's life and ministry.

23, David relates with rare enthusiasm the production of a great spectacular. He tells how he amassed a chorale of four thousand singers, accompanied by a great symphony orchestra playing instruments which David had especially made for the occasion. He then divided the singers into separate groups for descants and part singing, as well as antiphonal effects. He says the division was decided upon according to the sons of Levi; there was the Gershom choir, the Kohath choir, and the choir of Merari. And right there in the Temple of Jehovah, at the instruction of almighty God, the art of music broke forth with all its beauty, all its strength, and all its glory.

Francis Schaeffer, in his book, *Art and the Bible,** describes music that was produced in Hezekiah's day as "ten times greater than our twentieth-century concerts, with trumpets, cymbals, psaltries, harps, and all the various instruments of David . . . music upon music, art upon art . . . all pouring forth, all pointing up the possibility of creativity in praise of God, all carried to a high order of art at God's command."

And then he goes on to make this magnificent statement of the importance of music as an art form: "And when you begin to understand this sort of thing, suddenly you can begin to breathe, and all the terrible pressure that has been put on us by making art something less than spiritual suddenly begins to disappear. And with this truth comes beauty: and with this beauty a freedom before God."

For us Christians, redeemed by the work of Christ and living under the lordship of Christ, the arts and sciences do have an important place in our lives—and not just a peripheral one. Christ has not only saved our souls, but our minds and bodies as well. This means that He has lordship over the total person, including our culture and our creativity. A Christian must use these arts to the glory of God, as things of beauty to the praise of God. An art work can be a doxology in itself. I love the quote on the face page of Schaeffer's book: "The Christian is the one whose imagination should fly beyond the stars."

MUSIC IS A GIFT FROM GOD

Luther once said, with typical expressive candor, "If any man despises music, as all fanatics do, for him I have no liking; for music is a gift of God, not an invention of man."

Walter Savage Landor once said, "Music is God's gift to man, the

* © 1973 L'Abri Fellowship. Published by Intervarsity Press.

only art of heaven given to earth, and the only art of earth we take to heaven."

Listen to the lyric of Reba Rambo's wonderful song, "He Gave Me Music":*

> In the beginning, the day that God created man,
> He started passing out the gifts he thought everyone should have.
> To some he gave the gift to teach and some the gift to prophesy,
> To some he gave the gift to heal and others just to testify.
> But he gave me music; the gift was there when I was born.
> Yes, he gave me music, so I just have to sing his song.
> He gave me music, heavenly melody.
> He gave me music to communicate love and peace.
> He gave me music; He trusted His gift to me.
> So I just have to sing this song, for He gave the music to me.

I love the principle of stewardship regarding God's gifts set forth in the parable that begins in Matthew 25:14. Christ relates the story of the master who entrusted three servants with various sums of silver. The first two, who were given two talents and five talents, managed by good management and creative ingenuity to double the amounts they had been given. And they were promptly rewarded by being trusted with a much larger investment.

But the third servant, who received only one talent, buried it for safekeeping. But when he was called before the master to give an accounting, he was scathingly rebuked for misuse and misinvestment of the talent that had been placed in his keeping.

The master didn't say, "Tell me now, how much did you donate to charity?" He simply told him he was unprofitable, wicked, and lazy, and he had him thrown out. The one talent he had been given was taken from him and given to another who would use it creatively, and the poor guy spent the rest of his days as an outcast—a total failure.

That's pretty rough treatment. But remember, this is a parable. The story begins with these words: "This is an illustration of the kingdom of heaven."

You say, "What has this got to do with music?" And I say that stewardship is stewardship, and a gift is a gift. As surely as I am sitting

---

* "He Gave Me Music" by Reba Rambo and Dony McGuire. Copyright © by Lexicon Music, Inc., and It's-N-Me Music. International Copyright Secured. All Rights Reserved. Used by Permission.

here, God gave music to his people, both collectively and individually. Some of us have been entrusted with its creation, preservation, and renovation, and others have been charged with its propogation, exercise, and distribution. But both personally and collectively we are responsible for its use and reproduction, for it is one of heaven's most valued commodities.

MUSIC THE MINISTRY

That brings me to the topic at hand, for I believe that music the art and music the gift find their highest and noblest calling in music the ministry. The Bible says in Ephesians 5:19: "Talk with each other much about the Lord, quoting psalms and hymns and singing sacred songs, making music in your hearts to the Lord." And in Colossians 3:16: "Remember what Christ taught and let His words enrich your lives and make you wise; teach them to each other and sing them out in psalms and hymns and spiritual songs, singing to the Lord with thankful hearts."

Historians have stated, and I quote from the preface of Kenneth Osbeck's book, *Hymnology,* that "during the sixteenth century, Martin Luther won more converts to Christ through his encouragement of congregational singing than even through his strong preaching and teaching."

Of the eighteenth-century Wesley brothers, it was said that "for every person they won with their preaching, ten were won through their music."

Dwight L. Moody had his Ira Sankey. The two men met during a convention in Indianapolis, Indiana, in 1870, at which Moody was the guest speaker and Sankey was called upon to direct the music.

Their first meeting went like this: Moody shook Sankey's hand and queried, "Where are you from?"

Sankey answered, "From Pennsylvania."

Moody asked, "Are you married?"

Sankey responded, "I am."

Moody asked, "How many children do you have?"

Sankey said, "Two."

Moody asked, "What is your business?"

Sankey said, "I'm a government officer."

"Well," shot back Mr. Moody, "You'll just have to give it up."

And give it up he did, for Ira Sankey resigned his government position and moved to Chicago with his family to begin his fruitful evangelistic endeavors with Moody. He was mightily used of God through a ministry of music which was, no doubt, the basis for D. L. Moody's famous statement, "Singing does at least as much as preaching to impress the Word of God upon people's minds. Ever since God first called me, the importance of praise expressed in song has grown upon me."

Will Thompson, who wrote the music and lyrics to the great invitation song, "Softly and Tenderly," was also a great friend of D. L. Moody and visited him as he lay on his deathbed. As Mr. Thompson leaned close, Moody feebly whispered, "Will, I would rather have written 'Softly and Tenderly' than anything I have been able to do in my lifetime."

Billy Sunday had his Rodeheaver. In his book entitled *Twenty Years with Billy Sunday,* * Mr. Rodeheaver said, "Mr. Sunday loved a song with a lively lilt and rhythm. Our song service usually ran from thirty to forty minutes unless the tabernacle was filled before 7:30, in which case we'd start earlier and sometimes continue for a full hour. Usually we started off with some of the old, familiar hymns everybody could sing, then mix in some of the newer gospel songs which we would teach the people, interspersing these with a solo, a duet, or special numbers by the great chorus choir." It has been said the "many thousands of people all over the world and many thousands in heaven have gotten the challenge and inspiration that led them to God's Word through the music at the Billy Sunday campaigns."

Billy Graham has his George Beverly Shea, with whom he has been associated for over forty years. Of Bev, Billy says, "One of the characteristics that makes Bev Shea unique as a singer is that he sings a sermon." And on one occasion I heard Dr. Graham say, "It would be very difficult for me to preach without George Beverly Shea singing first."

And now a few words regarding excellence in the ministry of music. Thomas Hastings, who lived in the eighteenth century, has been credited as one of the men most instrumental in shaping the development of church music in the United States. He wrote the music for "Rock of Ages" and many other great hymns and Christian songs. Let me share a quote from Mr. Hastings showing that, even in the 1700s, Christian musicians endeavored to imbue their creative efforts with excellence. He said, "The homage that we owe almighty God calls for the noblest and most reverential tribute that music can render."

And now a few words regarding the effectiveness and relevancy of our music ministry. Never be afraid of a new song. We are admonished

* © MCMXXXVI Whitmore and Smith. The Rodeheaver Co. Owner.

ten times over from Psalms 33:2 to Revelation 14:3 to sing a new song. The message we have to share is timeless and unchanging, but if we are to communicate it to a changing world, the medium must be constantly changing. There are new concepts in rhythm, pitch, harmonization, and phrasing, as well as state-of-the-art technology in sound reproduction, not to mention the constant evolution in lyrical vernacular. All of these make it imperative to be acutely aware of these changes in our search for ways and means to stay relevant.

I once heard Dr. Joseph Bayley preach his famous sermon on "change for the church," in which he so eloquently reminds us that everything changes—everything, that is, but two unwavering, never-changing givens. One is God's provision for man: "Jesus Christ the same yesterday, today, and forever." The other is man's desperate need for God through the great redemptive process. These two things remain fixed and unchanging, but all else changes, even music—or perhaps *especially* music. And while we must treasure our rich heritage of the great old traditional music, we must never stop learning and creating, striving and experimenting, in our efforts to be effective communicators of the gospel through music.

Perhaps it is helpful to realize that the church has always had problems in keeping up with musical changes. Why, even in the 1700s and 1800s, when many of our "traditional" hymns were written, many of the hymn writers made use of popular secular melodies. And their combining of the unchanging message with the "pop" music of the day was sternly criticized.

Today, the musical "pop" style of the 1800s is what we call traditional and is one of the musical sounds that expresses that distinctive "otherness" of the church. It did not change through the years to take on this characteristic. It simply remained the same while other musical styles developed in society.

The same process occurred in the first half of the twentieth century, and in retrospect is now quite significant. Whatever the idiom, be it jazz, blues, ragtime, ballad, or march, the musical expressions at the beginning of this revolution all shared one common characteristic: They could not be identified as coming from within the church. (I had the pleasure/pain of introducing some of these forms.)

Intrinsic to the process was the combining of sacred words—God's unchanging message—and truly secular music, that is to say, music of the people or pop music. An important part of the dynamic in operation was the fact that the church was speaking with a kind of music generally thought of as "nonsacred."

By the late 1960s, the gap was beginning to develop again between the church sound and the sounds that were emerging as a new kind of entertainment music in the secular field. Thank God the young people forced a revolution of their own, as youth choirs cropped up by the thousands singing "Pass It On," "He's Everything to Me," "Tell It Like It Is," "Good News," and "Natural High," to the strumming of guitars and the beat of the drum.

And so it has been throughout the ages, and even to the present time. The ministry of music has been used providentially by a sovereign God to edify the saint, challenge the unbeliever, and to fan revival fires.

Longfellow said, "Music is the universal language of mankind." I say let's use this language to speak to mankind of God's magnificent redemption through Jesus Christ our Lord.